W0016306

Contents

Unit 1 Australia

▶ pp. 6–7

O* **1 Find the places**

a) Look carefully at the map on the front inside cover of your student's book. Then close the book and match the following places to the correct number or letter.

> South Australia · Victoria · New South Wales · Queensland · Northern Territory · Tasmania · Melbourne · Sydney · Western Australia · Brisbane · Perth · Darwin · Alice Springs · Adelaide · Cairns

1   Western Australia

2   Northern Territory

3   South Australia

4   Queensland

5   New South Wales

6   Victoria

7   Tasmania

A   Perth

B   Darwin

C   Alice Springs

D   Adelaide

E   Cairns

F   Brisbane

G   Sydney

H   Melbourne

b) Match the places to the states:

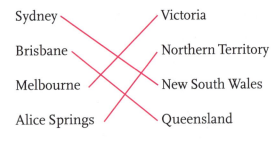

Sydney — Victoria
Brisbane — Northern Territory
Melbourne — New South Wales
Alice Springs — Queensland

INFO BOX

Australia has …
- only 21 million people but more than 150 million sheep.
- about 1,500 different kinds of spiders[1].
- the world's biggest cattle station.
- 40 different kinds of kangaroos.

Australia is …
- the sixth largest country in the world.
- one of the driest places in the world.
- 40% tropical, but with snow on the Snowy Mountains in NSW.

*O leichte Übung   [1] spider ['spaɪdə] Spinne

2 Welcome to Australia! ▶ *pp. 6–7*

Read Judith's blog on p. 6 of your student's book and complete the sentences in your own words. Then write one more sentence to give more information.

1 From the plane window Judith felt very small and a bit scared because she saw how huge and empty Australia was. The outback looked flat and endless.

2 When Judith landed in Melbourne, she got a shock because in Cologne it had been a hot day in summer. In Australia it was a cold day in winter.

3 School in Melbourne is different from school in Cologne for the following four reasons: The school year has four terms. The school day begins at 8.30 and ends at 3.15 every day. After school students do extracurriculars, then homework. So in Australia school fills the whole day.

4 During a five-day hike in the bush, a snake fell from a tree onto the arm of one of the girls. It scared everybody.

5 In their free time lots of Australian teenagers do sport and go surfing. They also love to go to 'barbies' (barbecues) and parties at their friends' houses.

Now you

Write notes about what you have learned from Judith's blog. Make two lists about: 1) Australia; 2) teenagers in Australia. Then write a paragraph each from your notes in your exercise book.

1 Australia: is huge, flat, has miles of red earth, …

2 Teenagers in Australia: have four school terms, school until 3.15 every day, learn how to surf, …

○ 3 REVISION   Describing a picture ▶ *p. 7 • SF (p. 126)*

*Look at picture 3 on p. 7 of your student's book. Why does it look strange? What's happening? Describe details of the scene in a paragraph. Use **in the foreground/background/middle, on the left/right**, etc.*

Picture 3 shows a man on a beach in Australia. He is dressed as Father Christmas , but he is wearing flip-flops. The man is standing in the foreground on the left in front of a Christmas tree, which is in the middle of the picture. On the right, on the left and in front of the tree there are some Christmas presents in gold, silver and red paper. Father Christmas is just putting a silver star on top of the tree.

In the background you can see the blue sky and the blue sea. On the right of the picture there are some swimmers.

> **INFO BOX**
>
> On beautiful Seventy-Mile Beach on Fraser Island (east coast) you can drive your car, jeep or bus or even land a small plane.

Test

4 Background File   Australia quiz   ▸ *pp. 8–9*

a) *Read pp. 8–9 of your student's book again. Then mark A, B or C. You need the letters in brackets in b).*

1 The capital of Australia is …

| A | Melbourne. (P) | B̶ | Canberra. (G) | C | Sydney. (D) |

2 The first Europeans landed in Australia in the … century.

| A | 14th (G) | B | 15th (I) | C̶ | 16th (E) |

3 In 1788 the British founded a colony in Port Jackson for …

| A | farmers from Britain. (L) | B̶ | convicts from Britain. (R) | C | pilgrims from Britain. (E) |

4 Australia was founded in …

| A | 1770. (S) | B | 1788. (T) | C̶ | 1901. (B) |

5 Today most immigrants to Australia come from …

| A | the USA. (O) | B̶ | Asia. (I) | C | Britain. (E) |

6 A big health problem in Australia is …

| A | pollution in the cities. (M) | B̶ | the ozone hole. (I) | C | dangerous animals. (E) |

7 Australia's population is mainly of … origin.

| A | American (E) | B | Asian (I) | C̶ | European (O) |

8 Which three animals are found only in Australia?

| A | Kangaroo, emu, lion. (U) | B̶ | Koala, emu, kangaroo. (A) |
| C | Koala, kangaroo, lion. (L) | | |

9 The Great Barrier Reef is … long.

| A | more than 2,000 miles (O) | B | 1,500 km (H) | C̶ | more than 2,000 km (S) |

10 The Great Barrier Reef has about … species of corals.

| A | 200 (P) | B̶ | 400 (N) | C | 1,500 (A) |

b) *If your answers are correct, you can put the letters in brackets in the right order to give you the name of a group of people:* ___Aborigines.___

◉* ## 5 LISTENING   Captain James Cook   ▸ *p. 9 • WB (p. 77)* 🎧 **2**

Test

a) *Listen carefully and write **T** (true) or **F** (false).*

1 James Cook had six brothers and sisters.   *F*

2 Cook became a sailor like his father.   *F*

3 He joined the Royal Navy[1] when he was 27.   *T*

4 He was sent by the British government to discover an unknown southern continent.   *T*

5 He made his first journey in a ship named the *Resolution*.   *F*

6 He claimed Australia for Britain on his second journey.   *F*

7 He was killed on a Hawaiian island.   *T*

WB, pp. 54–57

b) *Listen again and take notes (important dates, events). Use your notes to write a short biography of Cook's life. Write about 100 words in your exercise book.*

*◉ schwierige Übung   [1] Royal Navy [ˈrɔɪəl ˈneɪvi] *königliche Marine*

6 REVISION A trip to Oz (Tenses) ▶ p. 11 • GF (p. 155)

a) *Complete the dialogue with the correct simple past form of the verbs in brackets.*

Will Hi, Jay! When _did you get_ (you, get) back from Australia?

Jay Last Friday. We _had_ (have) a really good time. We even _went_ (go) on a hike into the bush.

Will Well, that must have been fun! _Did you see_ (you, see) any dangerous snakes or scary insects?

Jay Well, we _didn't see_ (not see) any, but I _was_ (be) pretty nervous all the

time. I _didn't sleep_ (not sleep) very well in the tent.

But nothing _happened_ (happen). We _spent_

(spend) the last few days in Sydney.

Will Great! _Did you do_ (you, do) the Bridge Climb?

Jay No, it _looked_ (look) too scary. But we _tried_ (try)

surfing on Bondi Beach. It _didn't look_ (not look)

difficult when the instructor _showed_ (show) us what to do, but I _spent_

(spend) more time in the water than on the surfboard, I'm afraid!

0506

b) *Imagine two friends have just come back from Australia. Write six questions that you would ask them about their holiday. Three questions should begin with a question word. Write in your exercise book.*

7 WORDS What do they mean? ▶ p. 11

a) *Explain these words. Use relative clauses with **who**, **which/that** or **where**.*

sleeping bag: A sleeping bag is something that you sleep in when you are camping.

sunscreen: Sunscreen is something that you put on your skin to protect it from the sun.

desert: A desert is a large area of dry earth where people don't usually live.

teenager: A teenager is a young person who is between 12 and 20 years old.

ancestor: An ancestor is a person in your family who lived many years ago.

emu: An emu is an Australian bird that can't fly.

0507 **instructor:** An instructor is a person who teaches you some kinds of sport or a skill.

b) *Choose four of the words in a) and use them in two sentences.*

If you go to the desert, you will need a lot of sunscreen.

Teenagers sometimes ask their parents about their ancestors.

8 WORDS   More than one meaning   ▸ p. 11

What do the underlined words mean in the following sentences? Write the German translation.

1 A Change at gate 5.   B Where can I <u>change</u> money?   C Aborigines <u>changed</u> the landscape.

  A _umsteigen_   B _wechseln_   C _verändern_

2 A Space isn't a problem in Australia.   B Move on two <u>spaces</u>.   C The Great Barrier Reef can be seen from <u>space</u>.

  A _Land, Platz_   B _Felder_   C _Weltraum_

3 A Do you have a £10 <u>note</u>?   B He sings the high <u>notes</u> very well.   C Take <u>notes</u>.

0608

  A _(Geld-)Schein_   B _Noten_   C _Notizen_

9 STUDY SKILLS   Charts   ▸ p. 11 • SF (p. 127)

Write about the two charts. What kind of charts are they? What do they show? What can you conclude? Use phrases from your student's book (p.10).

1 Reasons for visiting Australia (international visitors)

- Tourism 47%
- Friends 23%
- Business 17%
- Education 7%
- Work 2%
- Other 4%

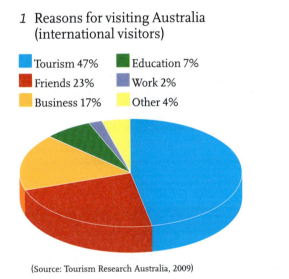

(Source: Tourism Research Australia, 2009)

2 Where visitors to Australia come from (in thousands)

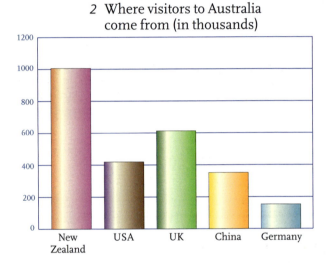

1 This is a _pie_ chart. *It shows what percentage of international visitors go to Australia and for what reasons. It is divided into six sections.* Tourism makes up the biggest section with 47% of all visitors. 23% go to visit friends. 17% go on business and 7% for education, but only 2% of all visitors go to work there. From these percentages we can see that the majority of international visitors (70%) goes to Australia on holiday.

2 This is a bar chart. It compares the numbers of visitors to Australia from different countries in thousands. It shows that a large majority of visitors comes from New Zealand. More visitors come from the UK than from the USA, and almost twice as many visitors come from the UK as from China. Of the five countries the smallest number of visitors comes from Germany. You can also see that there are about four times as many visitors from the UK as from Germany.

10 SPEAKING COURSE   Part 1: Hello! (Having a conversation)   ▶ p. 14 • WB (p. 80) 🎧 3

a) *Look in your student's book again (p. 14). Write phrases you could use in the different steps of a conversation.*
More than one phrase is possible.

Step 1: You want to start a conversation with somebody you don't know.
Hello!/Excuse me, …/Hi!

Step 2: You introduce yourself.

I'm … by the way./My name's …

Step 3: You start with a few general questions.

Have you ever …?/What about you? …

> **INFO BOX**
>
> There are many words and expressions that are unique to Australia. One is 'fair dinkum', which means 'real, true, genuine'. You will often hear the expression 'a fair dinkum Aussie', – a true Australian.

Step 4: You ask for help or information.

Can you tell me …?/Do you know where …? …

Step 5: You tell someone that you don't understand, or you ask someone to repeat something.

Sorry, I didn't get that./Can you say that again, please?/What does that mean? …

Step 6: You end the conversation.

Bye!/See you tomorrow./Thanks for your help …

b) *Ben is a student from the UK. It's his first day in Sydney. He wants to go to the beach, so he asks a girl on the*
street where he can buy some things that he needs. Complete the conversation with phrases from a). Then
listen to your CD (🎧 3) and check your answers. The CD gives only one possible answer.

Ben   Hello! Excuse me, …

Girl   Hi! Going to the beach?

Ben   Yes, but it's a bit too hot for me.
     My name is/I'm Ben, by the way.

Girl   Hi, Ben! I'm Lucy. Nice *to meet you* .
     You're from the UK, right?

Ben   Yes, I am. I live near London.
     Are you from here/Sydney?

Girl   Sure. I've lived here all my life. It's a great city.

Ben   This is my first day here. *Can you tell me where/Do you know where*
     I can get some sunscreen and a hat? I didn't think it would be so hot.

Girl   Well, there's a place that sells tourist stuff just round the corner on the left.
     Then you can slip, slop, slap.

Ben   Sorry, *I didn't get that* . What did you say? *Can you say that again* , please?

Girl   (*laughing*) Well, that's just what we say here – because of the sun. 'Slip! Slop! Slap!'

Ben   Oh. Well, *thanks for your help* . *Bye!*

c) *Write a new dialogue between Ben, who now wants to rent¹ a bike for the day, and a girl he meets on the*
beach in your exercise book. Use phrases from a) and ideas from b).

VB, pp.
8–69

0710
0711

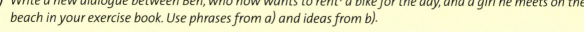
¹ rent *mieten*

11 WORDS Get it right! ▶ p. 15

Choose the correct word from the box and use it in the correct form to complete the sentences.

1 ride • go • drive : Jeannie lives in the middle of nowhere, so she can't __go__ anywhere by train or bus.

She __rides__ her horse and her dirt bike every day, but will she ever learn to __drive__ a car?

2 do • make • take : Rob __does__ lots of sport, but just now he's __taking__ a break from

surfing because he has to work hard for school. At the moment he's __making__ breakfast before he goes to the beach with his books.

3 than • as • when : Jeannie learned to ride a bike __as__ a small child, __when__ she was only

three. I think riding a dirt bike is more fun __than__ playing cricket.

4 need • take : Jeannie says the nearest town is 300 miles away. How often do they __need__

0811 to go there and how long does it __take__ to get there?

12 EVERYDAY ENGLISH WRITING (Writing an e-mail) ▶ p. 15 • WB (pp. 81–82)

You would like to know more about the sports that Australian teenagers play. Write to Rob. Make notes, then write your e-mail in your exercise book. Use paragraphs and topic sentences. Think of a good closing sentence.

Ideas:
> **skydiving** – how learn? expensive? how dangerous? • **surfing** – how long to learn? equipment expensive? • **cricket** – school sport? rules? • **Aussie rules football** – how different?

WB, pp. 63–67

> Dear Rob,
> I found your website really interesting and your pictures are great. I'd like to know more about ...

Now you

What are the advantages/disadvantages of living 'in the middle of nowhere'? Make notes in your exercise book and prepare a three-minute talk for class.

Ideas: free • clean air • quiet • nature[1] • animals • boring • friends • entertainment

13 REVISION (Verb + object + *to*-infinitive) ▶ p. 18 • WB (pp. 83–84)

*Make one sentence out of two. Use the underlined words (verb + object + **to**-infinitive).*

1 Tourists shouldn't climb Uluru. The Aborignes don't like it.

The Aborigines __don't like tourists to climb__ Uluru.

2 Visitors can ask questions about Aboriginal traditions. Aboriginal tour guides like that.

Aboriginal tour guides __like visitors to ask__ questions about Aboriginal traditions.

3 All white people should respect Aboriginal culture. The Aborigines want that.

The Aborigines __want all white people to respect Aboriginal culture.__

4 Tourists shouldn't take photos of some special parts of Uluru. Tour guides ask this.

0813 Tour guides __ask tourists not to take__ photos of some special parts of Uluru.

[1] nature [ˈneɪtʃə] Natur

14 REVISION   She didn't know what to do (Question word + to-infinitive) ▶ p. 18 • WB (p. 84)

Complete the text with a question word (what, who, how, where, which) + to-infinitive.

When Lena Müller arrived at Alice Springs airport her au pair family hadn't arrived. She waited half an

hour and she didn't know __what to__ do. She didn't know __how to__ use public phones in Australia,

and she didn't have any Australian change. She didn't know __which__ bus __to__ take to their house

and she wouldn't know __where/when to__ get off. She wondered __who to__ ask for help.

The woman at the information desk? But she didn't know __how to__ explain the situation in English.

Suddenly, a voice behind her said, 'Hey! You must be Lena. Sorry we're late. We had a problem with a

dangerous snake in our yard and we didn't know __where to__ look for it. We're not sure where it is

0914   now … But no worries, we'll show you __what to__ do if it's in your room …'

15 What to do in Alice Springs (to-infinitives instead of relative clauses) ▶ p. 19 • WB (p. 84)

Make the sentences shorter with a to-infinitive instead of a relative clause.

1   There are some really good tours that you can choose from.   … good tours __to choose from.__

2   There are lots of interesting places that you could visit.   … places __to visit.__

3   There are some good hotels that you could stay at.   … good hotels __to stay at.__

4   There are miles of fantastic outback that you can drive through.   … outback __to drive through.__

0915   5   There are so many new things that you can discover.   … new things __to discover.__

16 MEDIATION
Climbing Sydney Harbour Bridge (Spoken English to German) ▶ p. 19 • WB (p. 79) 🎧 4

a) *You are going to climb Sydney Harbour Bridge with your family.*
You call the Bridge hotline to find out answers to your parents'
questions. Read the questions first. Then listen carefully and take
notes.

1   Wie kommt man am besten zur Brücke?
2   Kann man mit dem Auto hinfahren?
3   Wann müssen wir dort sein?
4   Gibt es eine Vorbereitung?
5   Wie lange dauert der Aufstieg?
6   Gibt es Dinge, die wir nicht tun dürfen?
7   Was soll man anziehen?
8   Was geschieht, wenn das Wetter schlecht ist?

WB, pp.
70–71

b) *Answer your parents' questions in German.*

> **INFO BOX**
>
> When the bridge was opened in 1932 it was used by about 11,000 cars every day. Now the average is more than 150,000 cars a day!

17 WORDS   Word families   ▸ p. 19

a) *Write another word that belongs to the same word family. Write* **N** *(noun),* **V** *(verb) or* **A** *(adjective). Sometimes your new word may have the same form as the word given.*

comparison (N) _compare (V)_

race (dt. *Rasse*, N) _racist (A)_

protect (V) _protective (A)/protection (N)_

respect (V) _respect (N)/respectful (A)_

reaction (N) _react (V)_

connect (V) _connection (N)_

conclude (V) _conclusion (N)_

contrast (N) _contrast (V)_

b) *Use words from a) in the correct form and complete the text.*

For 60 years thousands of children of mixed _race_ were taken from their Aboriginal families

because of the government's _racist_ policy[1]. The stealing ended in 1970, but the government did

not say sorry. The Aborigines _reacted_ with sadness and anger[2]. For years they _concluded_

that the government was not sorry. The government did not apologize officially until 2008, but in

contrast to earlier years, Aboriginal culture and traditions are now more _respected_

1017 by the white population.

18 REVISION   WORDS Linking words   ▸ p. 19

Write a list of the linking words that you already know, then use them to complete the text below.

and, or, but, so, before, after, when, while, because, as, although, if

Although it stands in the middle of the hot Australian desert, Uluru is visited by thousands of tourists

from all over the world. The easiest way to get there is to fly to Alice Springs, _but_ you can also make

the long, dry journey by road through the outback. _Before_ you go to Uluru, it's a good idea to

find out what to do and what not to do there. _When_ visitors first see Uluru they are amazed at

its size and beauty. It's an unbelievable sight at any time of day, _but_ the best time is sunset

_if_ you want your visit to be a magical experience. Tourists stand in wonder[3] _as/while_

the rock changes from all colours of red and orange to deep blue. Because of their beliefs the

Aboriginal people don't like visitors to climb Uluru, _so_ instead of climbing the rock tourists

often walk round it. So far more than 30 people have died of a heart attack _while_ they were

climbing in the hot sun, because some visitors do the climb _although_ they are not fit enough.

1018

[1] policy ['pɒlɪsi] *Grundsatz, Politik*   [2] anger ['æŋgə] *Wut*   [3] wonder ['wʌndə] *Staunen, Wunder*

19 STUDY SKILLS Reading literature ▸ pp. 24–25 • SF (pp. 138–139)

a) *These words are important when you talk about literature. Find the correct definition and match.*

plot	the main people in the story
setting	comparisons and metaphors to create atmosphere
atmosphere	the action and events that take place in the story
characters	the place where and the time when the story takes place
imagery	the feeling created by the setting of the story

b) *In what ways can an author present his/her characters to the reader? Read pp. 24–25 in your student's book again. Then write a short paragraph. Use your own words.*

Characters are presented to the reader in different ways, for example by description. The author can

desribe what his/her characters look like, their age, how they dress, what they do or like, hate, etc.

The author can also show the reader what his/her characters are like by what they say and how they speak,

what they feel and think, how they adjust to situations, their attitude to people or things.

20 READING WORKING WITH THE TEXT In the outback ▸ pp. 20–24 • WB (pp. 77–78)

a) *Put the events of the story (pp. 20–24) in the correct order.*

Rusty the dog disappears.	4
Bill repairs the Dog Fence where an emu has hit it.	2
The Flying Doctor is called to fly Bill to hospital.	9
A black boar attacks Bill and Rusty and hurts them badly.	6
Bill and Colm drive into the Victoria Desert.	1
Colm shoots the boar.	7
Colm helps Bill by filling holes made by wombats.	3
Colm finds Rusty and helps Bill to save her.	5
Colm takes Bill and Rusty in the car to the cattle station to get help.	8

WB, pp. 58–62

b) *Creative writing. Write a new story with its setting in the Australian outback in your exercise book. Use the pictures and the following ideas.*

Two teenagers rent¹ a jeep and drive into the outback. They find a strange map that is marked with a cross … They want to find out what it means …

¹ rent *mieten*

Skills Check 1

1 LISTENING Summer vacation 🎧 5

You will hear a conversation between Dan and his sister Mel. Read the sentences first, then listen and tick A, B or C. You will hear the recording only once.

1 The conversation takes place ...

- [ ] A on a train to Brisbane.
- [x] B on a plane to Melbourne.
- [ ] C on a bus to Darwin.

2 Their arrival time is ...

- [ ] A 4.45.
- [x] B 14.45.
- [ ] C 14.54.

3 Why are Dan and Mel going there?

- [ ] A To go to summer camp.
- [ ] B To do a summer job.
- [x] C To visit family.

4 Mel and Ruth are ...

- [ ] A friends.
- [ ] B sisters.
- [x] C cousins.

5 During their vacation Dan and Mel are planning to ...

- [ ] A go shopping.
- [x] B do lots of sport.
- [ ] C do lots of sightseeing.

6 They have already been to the City Museum ...

- [ ] A twice.
- [x] B three times.
- [ ] C four times.

2 LISTENING A day in the life of ... 🎧 6

You will hear part of a radio interview with two firefighters from the Queensland Fire Service. Read the task below first, then listen to the recording. You will hear the recording twice.

a) *What do you hear about in the interview? Tick the correct box.*

- [ ] A koala rescue operation
- [ ] The history of bushfires in Queensland
- [x] Why bushfires start

b) *Tick true or false.*

	True	False
1 Bob has been a firefighter for 30 years.		✔
2 Steve had an office job with a company before he became a firefighter.	✔	
3 On average, Queensland gets 258 days of sunshine a year.		✔
4 In the fire season firefighters work round the clock and get very little sleep.	✔	
5 Bob flies a helicopter with waterbombing equipment.		✔
6 High temperatures and strong winds are natural causes of bushfires.	✔	
7 Eucalyptus forests burn easily because of the oil[1] in the leaves.	✔	
8 The public can't do anything to prevent bushfires.		✔
9 It's often difficult to make people leave their homes, although the fires are close.	✔	
10 The worst bushfires in recent[2] years were in Queensland in 2009.		✔
11 Bob remembers saving a little girl's cat from the garden of her ruined house.		✔
12 Steve really likes being a firefighter.	✔	

[1] oil [ɔɪl] Öl [2] recent ['riːsnt] *jüngst, aktuell*

3 READING Sydney for everyone

a) Look at the text quickly. What is it about? Tick a box.

☐ Sydney's beaches   ☐ Sydney's history   ✔ Sydney's sights

b) Look at the text a second time. What information does it give? Tick the correct boxes.

✔ Opening times   ☐ Prices   ✔ Sights information   ☐ How to get there

SYDNEY FOR EVERYONE

Start at The Rocks

The Rocks is the oldest part of Sydney. Historically, it is an area of great importance as it is here that Sydney was founded, when the first British convicts were sent here in 1788. Because of its well-preserved architecture from colonial times, it is often called Sydney's 'outdoor museum'. But today The Rocks combines historic buildings with trendy boutiques, souvenir shops, cafés, restaurants and a weekend street market. The Sydney Visitor Centre is here too, so it's a good place to start your visit. **Open** daily from 9.30 am to 5.30 pm.

Climb Sydney Harbour Bridge

This is one of Sydney's most popular tourist attractions, called the Coat Hanger by local people. It's easy to see why. Don't miss the challenge of the Bridge Climb for an unforgettable experience! The building of the bridge took about eight years. It was opened in 1932 and is used by about 150,000 vehicles daily. It takes about 80,000 litres of paint to paint the bridge once, and painting never stops. Did you know that the movie star Paul Hogan, better known as 'Crocodile Dundee', used to be a bridge painter before he became famous? **Opening times**: 7 am to 8 pm daily.

Visit Sydney's historic buildings

Visit Elizabeth Farm in Parramatta, Australia's oldest European building. Begun in 1793, the farm was the home of John and Elizabeth Macarthur, settlers from England who became sheep farmers and started Australia's wool export industry. The old house, its furniture and its gardens show visitors how they lived in the early 19th century. There are no guided tours. **Open** 9.30 am to 4 pm Fri. to Sun.

See a world-famous sight

The spectacular Sydney Opera House is situated in Sydney Harbour, surrounded by water on three sides. It was built by a Danish architect and was completed in 1973. Its design is a masterpiece of twentieth-century architecture and a world-famous sight. By the way, not only opera but also concerts, theatre and ballet are performed here. If you take the two-hour backstage tour, you can stand on the stage where stars like Pavarotti or Michael Bublé have performed, and find out stories from behind the scenes ... Oh, and be prepared to climb up 300 steps!

Visit Sydney Aquarium

Sydney Aquarium is one of the biggest in the world, with at least 6,000 fish, mostly Australian, and 650 different species. Don't miss the collection of sharks[1]. Some weigh as much as 300 kg. Visitors walk through underwater viewing tunnels to see marine life close up, so you can look a shark in the eye! **Opening times:** 9 am to 10 pm daily.

[1] shark [ʃɑːk] *Hai*

c) *Now read the text for details. Is the information true (T), false (F) or not in the text (N)? Tick the correct box.*

	T	F	N
1 The Rocks is an area of Sydney which reminds[1] visitors of Australia's colonial history.	✔		
2 Pilgrims from Britain arrived there in 1788.		✔	
3 There is a Rocks farmers' market on Fridays.			✔
4 Painting the Harbour Bridge is a never-ending job.	✔		
5 The Macarthurs were cattle farmers from England.		✔	
6 People call John Macarthur 'Father of the wool industry'.			✔
7 Sydney Harbour Bridge was started in 1924.	✔		
8 The Bridge is a railway bridge only.		✔	
9 Sydney Aquarium is home to 6,000 species of fish.		✔	
10 Sydney Aquarium is the world's second biggest.			✔
11 Sydney Opera House is near Sydney Harbour on a small island.		✔	
12 A Danish architect designed and built Sydney Opera House.	✔		
13 You can also see theatre productions at Sydney Opera House.	✔		
14 The backstage tour is one of the most popular tours.			✔
15 The backstage tour is not suitable[2] for people who can't climb.	✔		

4 WRITING   A blog or a summary

Complete task a) or task b).

a) *Write an interesting blog in English about your first day sightseeing in Sydney. You can take some facts from the text 'Sydney for everyone', but use your own words (about 150 words). Remember your writing skills.*

23 December

Hi, folks!

Yesterday I arrived in this most fantastic city! Here I am in ...

¹ remind [rɪˈmaɪnd] *jm. an etw. erinnern*   ² suitable [ˈsuːtəbl] *geeignet*

b) Write a summary of the following story in about 150 words in your exercise book.

A birthday surprise

It would be Nina's birthday soon. Her brother David and some friends had planned a birthday surprise for her – a trip to Kakadu National Park.

The group left early on their drive, laughing, joking and talking about what they might do there, walking, rock climbing, fishing, swimming in a freshwater billabong[1], picnicking by the river.

'You must be joking! What about the crocs?' said David, who was always careful and never did anything dangerous.

Cathy said that most of the crocs in the park were freshwater crocs, smaller and not aggressive like 'salties'.

Mike argued that thousands of visitors went to Kakadu, but only two or three died each year in a croc attack. But Mike loved an adventure. He never said no to anything scary.

'I agree,' said Nina, who had always been the wild one in the family. 'The park authorities take visitor safety seriously. Rangers check for crocs, even by helicopter. They can see them easily in the clear water. David, don't spoil[2] our fun! You're always scared of something. Enjoy yourself more! I always say: No risk, no fun!'

'So they've closed Twin Falls Gorge[3] and a few other places for swimming for no reason, have they? Why do you think there are crocodile warning signs everywhere? Nobody can give you a guarantee[4] that there will be no salties in the area, not even the rangers. There are no guarantees,' David continued in a serious voice.

'Come on, guys, that's enough. No more arguing. It's Nina's birthday tomorrow, and we're going to have a great time, eh, Nina?' said Mike laughing.

The rest of the day went well. In the evening they celebrated Nina's birthday round a campfire at the campsite. Nina was really happy.

The next day they made the short trip to the famous Jim Jim Falls. Nina wanted to see the beautiful plunge[5] pools. It was hot, and Mike was looking forward to a swim in the cool, clear water. The way there was a difficult climb over rocks. Mike and Nina loved rock climbing, so they soon left the others behind.

Suddenly David noticed that the two had disappeared. Nervously he shouted their names, but they were nowhere. 'This is crazy,' said David. 'We said we would all stay together.' Just then David fell and hurt his foot.

Cathy tried to calm him down, but she was worried too. 'They'll be back soon. We'll just wait here. You can't climb rocks anyway, if your foot hurts.' But after two hours Mike and Nina still hadn't come back. David felt sick with fear. The minutes seemed like hours. The waiting went on…

'Hey, you lazy guys! Where were you? It was great up at the plunge pool!' shouted a familiar[6] voice at last. It was Mike. They were back. David threw his arms round his sister. Nina didn't say much…

Safely back home after the trip, when she was alone with David, Nina said, 'David, I have to tell you about what happened up at the falls. A huge saltie suddenly appeared on the edge[7] of the lower pool only ten metres away. I was terrified, Mike too – but he would never admit[8] it. I couldn't move at first, but the croc came closer, so fast. We just dropped our stuff and ran away over the rocks – lucky that salties are bad climbers. We were too scared to go back, so we had to wait until it had gone – the worst two hours of my life. We could both have been eaten alive if we had jumped in the water. I'm so sorry about – you know. You were right – there are no guarantees. And David, please don't tell Mum and Dad…'

¹ billabong, *Seitenarm eines Flusses* ² spoil [spɔɪl] *verderben* ³ gorge [gɔːdʒ] *Schlucht* ⁴ guarantee [ˌgærənˈtiː] *Garantie*
⁵ plunge [plʌndʒ] *Tauch-* ⁶ familiar [fəˈmɪlɪə] *vertraut* ⁷ edge [edʒ] *Rand, Ufer* ⁸ admit [ədˈmɪt] *zugeben*

SPEAKING

MEDIATION

5 SPEAKING   Travelling 🎧 7

a) *At a travel agency in Australia you ask about tours to Uluru for your family. Listen and speak to the assistant: ask questions or form sentences in the pauses.*

Assistant   G'day! How can I help you? ...

1 Grüße ebenfalls und frage, was man bei der Uluru-Tour alles sehen kann.
2 Frage, wann die Tour losgeht.
3 Frage, wie lange die Tour dauert.
4 Frage, ob die Fremdenführer Aborigines sind.
5 Frage, ob man auf der Tour Frühstück bekommt.
6 Frage, wie viel die Tour kostet und was im Preis inbegriffen ist.
7 Sage, du möchtest die Tour für zwei Erwachsene und zwei Jugendliche für morgen buchen.

b) *Describe picture A or B: the background, the colours, the atmosphere. Say what the persons in the pictures are doing and how they maybe feel. Talk for about three minutes.*

I'd like to talk about picture A ...

c) *If you went to Australia, would you prefer to see the outback or to have a beach holiday? Say why. Talk for two minutes. You can record what you say.*

6 MEDIATION   Berlin tours

An Australian student would like to go to Berlin for a weekend and he asks you what you can see there. You find a brochure about Berlin tours. Write down the most important things for him in English in your exercise book.

Entdecken Sie Berlin mit Alpha Tours – wann und wie Sie wollen

Genießen Sie eine geführte Tour mit dem Bus, Fahrrad oder zu Fuß zu den vielen Sehenswürdigkeiten der Hauptstadt. Wir organisieren Touren jeder Art für große und mittlere Reisegruppen sowie für kleine Gruppen von 8 bis 12 Personen – und das jeden Tag! Wählen Sie Ihre spezielle Tour aus unseren vielen Angeboten aus!
Entdecken Sie u.a. folgende Highlights:
Regierungsviertel, Berliner Reichstag, Brandenburger Tor, Checkpoint Charlie, Mauerreste, Museumsinsel, Fernsehturm, Kaiser-Wilhelm-Gedächtniskirche, DDR Museum, Berliner Dom, Potsdamer Platz, Schloss Charlottenburg.

Wir bieten:
• moderne klimatisierte Reisebusse, neue bequeme Stadträder.
• Vormittags-, Nachmittags- und Abendtouren mit sämtlichen Eintrittsgeldern inklusive.
• genug Zeit für Fotostops und Erfrischungspausen bei allen Touren.
• bei Ganztagstouren ist auch ein Mittagessen enthalten.
• erfahrene, kundige Stadtführer/innen, die mehrere Fremdsprachen sprechen.
Besuchen Sie unsere Website, um Tourbeschreibungen, Preisinformationen, Adressen unserer Filialen und vieles mehr in Erfahrung zu bringen. Rufen Sie uns an oder kommen Sie ganz einfach vorbei!
Tel.: 030-529 487–0 / www.alphatoursberlin.com

How did you do?

Check your answers to the exercises on p. 87. Then answer the questions below with Yes or No.
If you tick No or would like some extra practice on that point, go to the exercise in your workbook
(▶ pp. 54–76).

	Yes	No	Exercise

1 LISTENING Summer vacation

1 Hast du dir vor dem Hören die Sätze gründlich durchgelesen? — ▶ 1, 2
2 Hast du die Detailfragen ohne Probleme beantworten können? — ▶ 3, 4
3 Konntest du die Sprecher mühelos verstehen? — ▶ 6

2 LISTENING A day in the life of ...

1 Konntest du nach dem 1. Hören beurteilen, um welches Thema es im Interview geht? — ▶ 1, 2
2 Hast du dir beim 1. Hören Notizen gemacht (Zahlen, Daten, Namen)? — ▶ 3, 5
3 Konntest du den australischen Akzent mühelos verstehen? — ▶ 7
4 Konntest du dem Sprechtempo mühelos folgen? — ▶ 8

3 READING Sydney for everyone

1 Konntest du schnell herausfinden, um was es in dem Text geht? — ▶ 10, 16a
2 Hast du nach Schlüsselwörtern (*key words*) gesucht, um Antworten zu finden? — ▶ 11
3 Konntest du die Antworten auf Detailfragen problemlos finden? — ▶ 13, 14
4 Hast du die Bedeutung unbekannter Wörter erschließen können? — ▶ 15, 16b

4 a) WRITING A blog

1 Hast du deine Ideen mithilfe eines *brainstorming* gesammelt und dazu Notizen gemacht? — ▶ 17
2 Hast du einige der 5 Ws am Anfang deines Textes berücksichtigt? — ▶ 18
3 Hast du Informationen aus Exercise 3 benutzt und mit eigenen Worten beschrieben? — ▶ 31, 32
4 Hast du passende Adjektive für deine Beschreibungen benutzt? — ▶ 35
5 Hast du hauptsächlich das *simple past* benutzt? — ▶ 30
6 Hast du deine Wortstellung (z.B. in Nebensätzen) überprüft? — ▶ 37
7 Hast du *linking words*, z.B. *but, after, before, while, because, although, so* benutzt? — ▶ 32, 33
8 Hast du deine Rechtschreibung/Grammatik überprüft und deine Fehler korrigiert? — ▶ 38

4 b) WRITING A Summary

1 Hast du die wichtigsten Ereignisse erkannt und dazu Notizen gemacht? — ▶ 17
2 Hast du die 5 Ws am Anfang deiner Summary berücksichtigt? — ▶ 18
3 Hast du die wichtigsten Ereignisse mit eigenen Worten wiedergegeben? — ▶ 19, 31, 32
4 Hast du direkte Rede sowie Beschreibungen weggelassen? — ▶ 19a+b
5 Hast du den Unterschied zwischen dem *simple present* und *present progressive* beachtet? — ▶ 29
6 Hast du deine Wortstellung (z.B. in Nebensätzen) überprüft? — ▶ 37
7 Hast du *linking words*, z.B. *but, after, while, because, although, so* benutzt? — ▶ 32, 33
8 Hast du deine Rechtschreibung/Grammatik überprüft und deine Fehler korrigiert? — ▶ 38

5 a) SPEAKING Travelling

1 Hast du problemlos passende Fragen mit *do/does* oder mit Fragewörtern bilden können? — ▶ 23
2 Hast du in den Pausen schnell genug die passenden Fragen stellen können? — ▶ 24b, 25c
3 Hast du die notwendigen Vokabeln gewusst? — ▶ 24a

5 b) SPEAKING Travelling

1 Hast du bei der Bildbeschreibung Ortsangaben wie z. B. *on the right/left* usw. benutzt? — ▶ 24
2 Hast du Dinge, die die Personen gerade tun, mit dem *present progressive* beschrieben? — ▶ 29
3 Hast du die Atmosphäre der Bilder mit passenden Adjektiven beschrieben? — ▶ 25, 35
4 Hast du wichtige Vokabeln für die Bildbeschreibung gewusst? — ▶ 24a

6 MEDIATION Berlin tours

1 Hast du beachtet, mit eigenen Worten nur das Wesentliche weiterzugeben bzw.
nicht alles wörtlich zu übersetzen? — ▶ 26
2 Hast du (falls nötig) für unbekannte Wörter Umschreibungen benutzt (*paraphrasing*)? — ▶ 34

Unit 2   The road ahead

◎ 1 WORDS   Planning the road ahead ▶ *pp. 32–33*

a) *Read pp. 32–33 of your student's book again. Find collocations and match the words below.*

work | pass | inherit | become | have | make | get | graduate | start

🖥 **1801**

exams | hard | a millionaire | qualifications | from university | a fortune | kids | a career | a difference

b) *Look at the pictures of Marcia, Andy and Trish taken six years after the young people left school. Which road did they take? Imagine what they say about their past, present and future. You can use phrases from a).*

Marcia   Andy   Trish

Marcia: Well, I took the career road. I worked hard at school, passed my exams, graduated from university, then I started a career at a bank. I have a great job in the City now. And I hope to become a project manager next year, maybe in Singapore or Hong Kong.

Andy: I decided against a career. I didn't go to university, but I travelled around the world for a year and met lots of interesting people. And I did volunteer work in four countries. I live in Africa now and I work for an organization which wants to help people. I always wanted to do something useful and make a difference.

Trish: I always planned to become a doctor, and I did. But I found the right partner and now I'm going to have our first child soon. Maybe I'll go back to my job in a year or two, but I'll be happy to have kids and be a good mum too. Money and success in your job are not the only things that make you happy.

2 WORDS   Looking ahead   ▶ p. 35

a) *Complete what the teenagers say with words from the box.*

A-levels • civilizations • *goals* •
in charge of • qualifications •
scientist • settle down • university

1

Whatever *goals* we
have for the future, we need some
good *qualifications* first.

4

Maybe I'll travel
round the world to see faraway
countries and *civilizations* .

2

My first step will
be to get some good
grades in my *A-levels* so
that I'll be able to get a place
at *university* .

5

I want to travel
around for a few years, but
as soon as I find the right partner
I'll *settle down* .

3

I see myself as a
top businesswoman one day,
maybe *in charge of* my own
fashion company.

6

I'm very
interested in science and
research. Maybe I'll be a famous
scientist one day.

1902

b) *What are the advantages of planning your 'road ahead'? What are the disadvantages? First make notes using phrases from a). Then write a paragraph each in your exercise book.*

3 WORDS   Personal qualities   ▶ p. 36

a) *What kind of person are you? What do others think? Complete the sentences with words from the boxes.*

a bit • quite • very • (not) always •
sometimes • usually

annoying • calm • careful • confident • energetic • flexible •
funny • good at • hard-working • helpful • honest •
interested in • keen on • musical • nervous •
noisy • organized • practical • punctual • quiet •
reliable • serious • sporty • tidy

1 I think my friends would describe me as _____

_____

2 I think my family would describe me as _____

_____

3 Maybe my teachers would say I'm _____

1903

_____

b) *If an interviewer said to you 'Tell me about yourself,' what would you say? Think carefully, then prepare your answer in a few sentences. Write them in your exercise book.*

4 SPEAKING COURSE Part 2:

Excuse me, ... (Asking for, confirming, giving information) ▶ *p. 37* • *WB (pp. 80–81)* 🎧 8,9

a) *Asking for information. / Being polite.* How could Jonas sound less direct, more polite and more friendly? Rewrite his sentences. There is more than one suitable answer.

1 *Jonas:* Hello. I want to go to Windsor. How do I get there?

<u>Excuse me. I'd like to go to Windsor. Do you think you could / Could</u>
<u>you tell me how to get there?</u>

2 *Jonas:* Where can I get a bus to Windsor?

<u>Excuse me, could you tell me where I can get a bus to Windsor,</u>
<u>please?</u>

3 *Jonas (in train):* Can you close the window?

<u>Excuse me, would you mind closing the window, please?</u>

4 *Jonas:* I want to do a tour of the castle. When does the next tour leave?

<u>Excuse me. I'd like to do a tour of the castle. Could you tell me when the next tour leaves?</u>

5 *Woman (in train):* Are you on holiday here? *Jonas:* Yes. <u>Yes, I am (actually).</u>

6 *Woman:* And did you enjoy the tour of the castle? *Jonas:* Yes. <u>Yes, I did. Very much. It was really</u> <u>interesting.</u>

7 *Woman:* Have you been to London before? *Jonas:* No. <u>No, I haven't. This is my first time. But I'm sure</u> <u>I'll come again.</u>

b) *Confirming information.* Listen (🎧 8) to the conversation at the train station. Which phrases does Elias use to confirm the information he is given? Write seven more phrases.

<u>Is that right?   And can I just confirm the directions?   I should go down here, ...</u>

<u>Have I got that right?   So I should ask for ...   Could you just repeat that, please?   So that's Mrs ...</u>

<u>Have I got that now?</u>

c) *Giving information.* Amina is having a phone interview for a summer job with a tour company in London. They need someone to answer telephone enquiries[1] from German tourists in German.

WB, pp. 68–69

1 First listen (🎧 9) carefully to the interview, especially Amina's parts.

2004

2 Now it's your turn to be interviewed. Listen to the interviewer's questions and give suitable answers in the pauses. You can take ideas from Amina's interview. Remember to be polite.

[1] enquiry [ɪnˈkwaɪəri] *Anfrage*

5 Extra Blue box: Negative prefixes ▶ *p. 37, p. 192*

Complete the interview tips with the negative form of the adjective in brackets. Guess or check the meaning of any word you don't know in your dictionary. You can also use your dictionary to find out which negative prefix you need.

1 Interviewers don't like applicants to be __unpunctual__ (punctual). If you're going to be late, call

the company and say why. It's very __impolite__ (polite) to arrive late without an explanation.

2 While you're waiting, you often have to fill in a form. Do it as well as you can, even if you think it asks

for __unnecessary__ (necessary) information. Write clearly. Most interviewers find __illegible__

(legible) handwriting extremely annoying. Don't give __incorrect__ (correct) or __inexact__
(exact) information.

3 Answer all the interviewer's questions, even if you think some of them are __unimportant__

(important) or __irrelevant__ (relevant).

4 Think carefully before you speak. If you have to give reasons, never use __illogical__ (logical)
arguments.

5 Don't be negative about any part of the job description. The interviewer may think you're

__inflexible__ (flexible) or even __unable__ (able) to do the work.

6 Remember, if the interview goes badly, don't feel __inadequate__ (adequate). You were just

__unlucky__ (lucky).

2105

6 REVISION   Luke's dad wants him to ... (Infinitive constructions) ▶ *p. 40 • WB (pp. 83–84)*

a) *Luke doesn't really know what he wants to do next year. What do other people want him to do?*

1 Dad	'Stay on at school and go to university.'	4 Girlfriend	'Stay at home and get a job in a bank.'
2 Mum	'Work hard and get good A-levels.'	5 Best friend	'Follow your dream and become a
3 Brother	'Do volunteer work abroad for a year.'		racing driver!'

1 Luke's dad __wants him to stay on at school and go to university.__

2 His mum expects __him to work hard and get good A-levels.__

3 His brother told __him to do volunteer work abroad for a year.__

4 His girlfriend wants __him to stay at home and get a job in a bank.__

5 His best friend told __him to follow his dream and become a racing driver.__

b) *Read Luke's questions on the right. Then complete the sentences with a question word + to-infinitive.*

1 Luke doesn't know __what to do next year.__

2 He can't decide __when to leave school.__

3 He doesn't know __what kind of job to train for.__

2106

4 He doesn't know __whose advice to take.__

> 1 What shall I do next year?
> 2 When shall I leave school?
> 3 What kind of job shall I train for?
> 4 Whose advice[1] shall I take?

[1] advice [əd'vaɪs] *Rat, Ratschlag*

7 Blue box: Same verb, different meaning   ▶ p. 40, p. 195

a) *Some students are talking about their interview experiences. Complete what they say with a **to**-infinitive or a gerund.*

1 I'll never forget ___going___ (go) to my first interview. I was terrified.

2 I almost forgot ___to say___ (say) 'thank you' before I left.

3 I went on ___talking___ (talk) about my hobbies for a long time. Not a good idea!

4 I knew I was doing OK when the interviewer went on ___to talk___ (talk) about money.

5 I tried ___to change___ (change) the subject when the interviewer asked a question I couldn't answer.

6 I wish people would stop ___telling___ (tell) me what to do.

b) *What do you remember doing in the past? What must you remember to do next week? Write three sentences each in your exercise book.*

2207 *I remember falling off a horse when I was eight. / I must remember to buy concert tickets next week.*

⬤ 8 STUDY SKILLS Writing a formal letter   ▶ p. 41 • SF (p. 146) • WB (pp. 81–82)

You are planning to do a language course in Oxford for three weeks during your summer holidays. Someone has given you the address of a nice place to stay. Write a formal letter to the house owner, Ms Claire Harris, 8 Broad Street, OX 1 3AP. For help you can use the phrases in the box and your student's book (p. 146). Write in your exercise book or use a computer.

1 Tell her what you would like (room with breakfast, maybe evening meal).
2 Give the dates of your stay.
3 Ask questions (how much it would cost per week, etc.).
4 Tell her about yourself (your level of written/spoken English, what kind of person you are, interests).

...
I am planning to do a language course in Oxford
and need accommodation for three weeks from ...
to ..., if possible with ... / I would be grateful if ... /
I am ... years old and have studied English for ...
years. / My level ... / I look forward ... /
Yours sincerely ...

WB, pp. 63–67

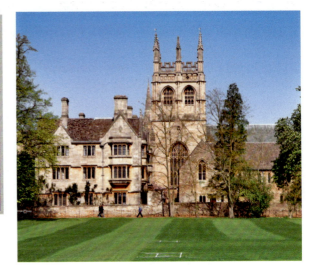

9 LISTENING   Phone calls   ▸ p. 41 • WB (p. 77) 🎧 10

Mrs Holby is a busy manager. Ben, her assistant, writes the times of her appointments and interviews in an appointments diary. Listen to the telephone calls, and write the necessary changes in the diary.

Monday	Tuesday	Wednesday	Thursday	Friday
~~10.30 Interview: Ms Jane Morton~~	10.15 ~~Mr D. Thomas, (Bell Electronics)~~ *10.30 Mr Tim Brown*	8.30 Dentist's appointment	9.30 Presentation	*8.30 Interview:* *Ms Jane Morton*
		11.00 Interview: Ms Maria Langton		*11.00 Dentist's* *appointment*
	2.30 Interview: Mr Peter Marlow	*2.00 Interview:* *Mr S. Rogers*	2.30 Visit to MPR Software, Harrow	~~2.00 Interview: Mr S. Rogers~~

WB, pp. 54–57

10 REVISION   After school (Gerunds as subject and object)   ▸ p. 42 • WB (pp. 84–85)

Complete the sentences with your own ideas. Use gerunds.

1   When I leave school, I'll really enjoy _____

2   _____ is something I've always wanted to do.

3   I can't really imagine _____

2310   4   I prefer _____ to _____ so that will be important when I apply for a job.

11 REVISION   A newspaper ad (Gerunds after prepositions)   ▸ p. 42 • WB (pp. 84–85)

Write a job advertisement with words from the boxes. There can be more than one possibility.

Join us as our new PROJECT MANAGER
We are a leading London IT company looking for someone who

• is tired   *of doing routine work*

• is bad   *at working alone*

• is good   *at organizing*

• is interested   *in setting up a new project*

• is used   *to making decisions*

• is keen   *on travelling*

If you are afraid   *of missing a great opportunity*,

call Sam Fletcher on 02072 455325 for more details.

of (2x) • at (2x) • on • in • to

travel • organize •
set up a new project •
do routine work •
make decisions •
work alone •
miss a great opportunity

2311

12 MEDIATION   US high school programs   ▶ p. 43 • WB (p. 79)

You would like to participate in an American high school program, but your parents aren't too happy about it. You found this information on a website. Tell your parents the important facts in German. Make notes first.

An academic year at an American high school

Who can apply?
If you are a foreign student 15 to 18 years of age, you may apply for a place in the academic program of an American high school. You should have good school grades and a good level of everyday English. All applicants will be interviewed in their own country, where they will also take a test in English.

School programs
US school classes start in August and finish in June. You will choose your schedule from a wide range[1] of academic subjects which include Math, English, Science, US History, Business, Industrial Design and PE. Additionally, you will choose extracurriculars. These may be different from school to school, but will usually include sports, music, drama, volunteer work and environmental projects. Your school will expect you to take part in all aspects of high school life.

What does the program price include?
You will stay with an American host family and will study at a local high school, often together with students from your host family. On arrival in the US you will be met at the airport and will be taken to your host family. You will have your own room and will eat with the family in the evenings and on weekends. The program price also includes your school registration fees[2] and educational school trips.

What extra costs will I have to pay?
Not included in the price are application fees, your travel/flights to the US, your travel insurance[3], medical insurance, transport to and from school, school books and school lunches.

WB, pp. 70–71

13 WORDS   Word families   ▶ p. 43

Complete with a word from the same family as the word in brackets. If you need a verb, use the correct tense.

Simon had read an __advertisement__ (advertise) for a summer job with a sports company. He decided

to send an __application__ (apply) to the manager, who invited him to an interview.

On the day of the interview Simon dressed __suitably__ (suitable) and arrived on time.

He saw that there were six other __applicants__ (apply) for the job, but he tried not to be nervous.

The manager asked Simon about his free-time __activities__ (active) and he seemed to be

very __interested__ (interest). Simon showed that he was an __organized__ (organize)

and __energetic__ (energy) person who loved sport. The manager also asked Simon about

his __strengths__ (strong) and weaknesses.

Simon hopes that he was able to __impress__ (impressive) the manager and that he will be

2413 the __successful__ (success) candidate.

---

[1] range [reɪndʒ] *Auswahl*   [2] registration fee [ˌredʒɪˈstreɪʃn fiː] *Anmeldegebühr*   [3] insurance [ɪnˈʃʊərəns] *Versicherung*

14 READING WORKING WITH THE TEXT
How to be a teenage millionaire ▸ pp. 46–48 • WB (pp. 77–78)

a) *Put the events of the story (SB pp. 46–47) in the correct order. Write the numbers 2–8 in the boxes.*

She bought the address whateverlife.com with the money. .... `3`

Ashley started to design websites when she was nine years old. .... `1`

She got her first cheque from an advertising company. .... `5`

Her mother lent her $8 to buy a domain name. .... `2`

Big advertising companies started to get interested in her website. .... `4`

She wants to study design in her dream city, New York. .... `8`

She left school before her 16th birthday. .... `6`

She had a problem with a friend who was working for her. .... `7`

b) *What do you know about Ashley? Tick the correct answers.*

1 She's determined and ambitious. ✔

2 She earns money by selling her designs. ☐

3 She doesn't miss school. ☐

4 She believes in herself. ✔

5 She has a strict set of rules for people who work for her. ✔

6 She's artistic and hard-working. ✔

7 She lives the normal life of a teenager. ☐

8 Her business brings in about $700 a month. ☐

c) *If Ashley was in your school class, how would you and your classmates probably feel about it? Answer the questions in a few sentences each. Give reasons for your answers. Use your exercise book.*

1 Would Ashley be a classmate just like all the other classmates?

   I think class relations would be just the same as before Ashley became rich. First, … / I don't think Ashley would be a classmate like the other classmates …

2 Would you want to work for Ashley? Why (not)?

   I wouldn't want to work for Ashley … / Yes, maybe … / Why not …

3 Ashley would be different from all your other classmates because of her money. Do you think this might lead to problems in the class?

   Yes, maybe. Being Ashley's friend might … / No, I don't think so because …

WB, pp.
8–62

● *d)* Extra *Do internet research to find another teenage millionaire and describe how he/she started a business. Maybe you can find parallels to Ashley's story. Write notes in your exercise book. Then tell the class about the teenage millionaire's story.*

INFO BOX
A UK teenage millionaire In 2002, when he was only 14, Fraser Doherty from Edinburgh started earning lots of money – in the kitchen. He used his grandmother's secret recipe[1] to make healthy jam[2] without sugar. Everybody loved it, so he decided to sell it at a local market for extra pocket money. Soon he had to rent a factory and employ people to make it. Now he sells his famous jam in large supermarket chains throughout the UK.

[1] recipe ['resəpi] *Kochrezept*   [2] jam [dʒæm] *Marmelade*

15 **Which verb? Which form?** (Activity verbs and state verbs) ▶ p. 49 • GF (p. 160)

a) Put the verbs in the box into three groups. Check your answers on p. 49 of your student's book.

> belong • have • know • look • *make* • play • seem • think • work

These verbs express …

1 **an activity**: they are used in the simple and in the progressive form ▶ *make, play, work*

2 **a state**: they are used only in the simple form ▶ *belong, seem, know*

3 **an activity or a state**: they are used in the simple form (for a state) or in the progressive form

(for an activity) ▶ *have, look, think*

b) Choose the correct form (simple or progressive) of the verb in brackets.

1 Meera *is thinking* (think) seriously of going abroad to do volunteer work after school.

2 She *knows* (know) that a year abroad will look good on her CV.

3 She also *thinks* (think) that volunteer work will be good for her.

2615 4 At the moment she *is looking* (look) at websites of volunteer work in South America.

16 **WORDS** **Good advice** (Phrasal verbs) ▶ p. 49

⊙ *a) Zainab has applied to university. Before her first interview her family and friends give her lots of advice. Use a phrasal verb from the box to complete what they say.*

> calm down • fill in • freak out • *put on* • sit down • think about • turn off • write down

1 Don't *put on* too much make-up, and wear something suitable!

2 Even if you're very nervous, *calm down* before the interview.

3 Don't *sit down* until the interviewer offers you a seat.

4 Don't forget to *turn off* your phone before you go into the interview room.

5 *Fill in* all the forms correctly.

6 *Think about* what they might ask you about your subjects.

7 *Write down* important information about the course.

8 Don't *freak out* if they ask you questions you can't answer!

2616
2617
2618 *b) Which pieces of advice do you think are the most important? Give reasons.*

How well can you do these things?

	Very well	OK	Practise!

LISTENING AND READING SKILLS: I can...

... understand longer conversations and longer written texts, e.g.
In the outback (SB pp. 20–24). ☐ ☐ ☐

... understand and find detailed information from what I hear or read.
(e.g. details about Ashley's business, SB pp. 46–47). ☐ ☐ ☐

... understand the Australian accent without difficulty (e.g. Rob talking about
sports, SB p. 13). ☐ ☐ ☐

SPEAKING AND WRITING SKILLS: I can...

... start a conversation with someone I don't know. ☐ ☐ ☐

... ask, confirm and give information in English. ☐ ☐ ☐

... ask and answer typical questions at a job interview. ☐ ☐ ☐

... write an e–mail to ask for information. ☐ ☐ ☐

... write my CV with the correct format. ☐ ☐ ☐

... write a formal letter of application and a formal letter asking for
information, in a suitable style and format. ☐ ☐ ☐

MEDIATION SKILLS: I can...

... report the most important facts from conversations or written texts,
both from German into English and from English into German. ☐ ☐ ☐

... use synonyms or paraphrasing for words and phrases I don't know. ☐ ☐ ☐

TOPICS: I have learned...

... about Australia's geography, history, animals, natural sights (e.g.
the outback, Uluru), the School of the Air, the Flying Doctor Service. ☐ ☐ ☐

... about Aboriginal culture and history, e.g. 'the Dreaming' and 'the stolen
generations'. ☐ ☐ ☐

... how to talk about work experience and qualities needed for different jobs. ☐ ☐ ☐

... how to write a job application and present myself at an interview. ☐ ☐ ☐

STUDY AND LANGUAGE SKILLS: I know...

... how to use an English grammar. ☐ ☐ ☐

... how to create visual aids and use them in presentations. ☐ ☐ ☐

... how to talk and write about statistics using tables, bar charts and pie charts. ☐ ☐ ☐

... how to talk about plot, setting, atmosphere and characters in literary texts. ☐ ☐ ☐

HOW I COULD IMPROVE MY ENGLISH SKILLS: I could...
(e.g. work through parts of Skills Check 1 again, revise the unit vocabulary lists...)

_____

_____

_____

Skills Check 2

1 LISTENING First day at work 🎧 11

You are going to hear Jenna talking about her first summer vacation job. Read the task first, then listen and tick A, B or C. You will hear the recording twice.

1 Jenna got her first summer vacation job in a …

- [ ] A clothes store.
- [x] B shoe store.
- [ ] C designer jeans boutique.

2 She wanted to work there because …

- [x] A she loves shoes.
- [ ] B she couldn't get any other job.
- [ ] C the store sold shoes for teenagers.

3 Jenna got the job there because …

- [ ] A she had work experience.
- [x] B they needed someone quickly.
- [ ] C she was the only applicant.

4 The first customer[1] bought shoes in …

- [x] A brown and black.
- [ ] B black and blue.
- [ ] C blue and brown.

5 The customer paid … for two pairs of shoes.

- [ ] A 155 dollars
- [x] B 310 dollars
- [ ] C 410 dollars

6 Jenna didn't know the correct price because …

- [ ] A someone told her the wrong price.
- [x] B there was no price on the shoes.
- [ ] C the price on the box was wrong.

7 When Jenna couldn't find shoes for the second customer, she …

- [ ] A asked the manager.
- [ ] B showed the customer different shoes.
- [x] C waited in the store room[2] until the customer had gone.

8 Jenna thought it would be unprofessional to …

- [x] A say she couldn't find the shoes the customer wanted.
- [ ] B ask how the system in the store room worked.
- [ ] C hide in the store room.

2 READING Jobs

a) Look at the five texts quickly. What are they about? Tick a box.

Young people describing a job they would like to do .... [ ]

Young people describing work experience that they have done .... [ ]

Young people describing jobs that they do .... [✓]

b) Read what the young people say. Look at the pictures on the next page. Which picture matches which description? Write A–F in the boxes. There is one picture more than you need.

1 **D** I work outside half of the time. I don't mind because there's usually something going on. And we work in twos on the street, so there's always a partner to talk to. We are often called to a traffic accident, a fight or a robbery in the area. I prefer it to sitting in the office writing up reports, but we have to do that too. There's some routine, but my job is much better than a nine-to-five job, and it's surprising how much crime there is in a small town. We're always busy. It's never boring.

2 **A** I love my job, though it isn't easy. You have to work really hard, and the pay is not good. We work shifts. I often have the night shift, which is quite hard because you're mostly alone, so it's difficult if there's an emergency. I always hope nothing will happen when I'm doing a night shift. We have to know a lot. It's a very responsible job and we mustn't make mistakes. We have to be exact in our work, punctual, reliable, caring and always friendly to our patients.

[1] customer [ˈkʌstəmə] *Kunde/-in*   [2] store room *Lager*

3 B In my job you have to be calm and organized and you have to be good in a team. I work with my boss and his partner. I always have to be punctual and reliable, but that's no problem. I had to learn a lot and do exams, and I'm still training, so I don't do operations myself yet. I'm glad that we can help old ladies and children when their pets are ill. But we also help farm animals, cows, sheep, horses. You don't have to mind getting your hands dirty. It's a good feeling being able to help and save lives.

4 F I'm an outdoor person. I definitely couldn't work in an office all day sitting at a desk and looking at a computer. I work for a company in town, but our projects are everywhere in the area, sometimes they're really big projects, office blocks or industrial parks. My job isn't very nice in winter when it's cold and it rains a lot. You have to be fit and quite strong. We carry heavy[1] building materials and we start early. It's nice to look at a beautiful new building and know that you were part of it.

5 E This is my second year as a trainee. It's hard work and I had to start from the bottom, cleaning floors and preparing vegetables – pretty boring. At first I learned all the standard dishes that are always on the menu, but I really enjoy being artistic with food and creating my own dishes. I hope to have my own restaurant one day.

A

Lauren

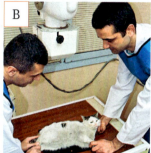
B

Adam

C

Penny

D

Lucy

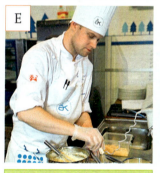
E

Nick

F

Sam

c) Write the correct name.

1 Who would like to own his own business? — *Nick*

2 Who likes being part of a big project? — *Sam*

3 Who doesn't like working night shifts? — *Lauren*

4 Who spends about 50% of working time outdoors? — *Lucy*

5 Who has completed one year of training? — *Nick*

6 Who assists at operations? — *Adam*

7 Who hates office work? — *Sam*

8 Who does heavy work and has to be fit? — *Sam*

[1] heavy ['hevɪ] *schwer*

WRITING

3 WRITING   A formal letter

An English friend sends you an advert from the Cornish Daily Post advertising holiday jobs in hotels in Cornwall. You are interested and would like more information. Write a formal letter to the manager and ask about the following:

- *what kind of hotel work is available*
- *where the hotels are*
- *hours, pay, free time*
- *accommodation, meals.*

Give information about yourself. Say why you would like to work in Cornwall, when you would be free and how many weeks you would like to stay. Write about 120 words. Make notes below, then write the letter on the computer.

Holiday jobs in Cornwall

We have a number of jobs for German-speaking students who would be interested in working in our hotels for 6–8 weeks in summer.
Please send your application with CV in English to:
George Sutton
Cornish Hotels
139 Sutton Road
Bude, EX23 0BA

4 WRITING   Your CV

Now write your CV to send with your application. Think about which information to include (personal and contact details, education, qualifications/skills, etc.). Present the information in a logical order. Remember to include a short personal statement. Make notes below, then write your CV on the computer.

CURRICULUM VITAE

5 WRITING   An informal letter

Write an informal letter to your English friend telling him/her that you have applied for a job in Cornwall. Say why the job interests you and think about positive and negative things. One good thing may be that you could visit your friend in Cornwall. Brainstorm your ideas first (mind map, list). Write about 150 words in your exercise book.

6 SPEAKING　Jobs and work experience

a) *Look at the pictures and describe the jobs. Compare the advantages and disadvantages of the two jobs. What are the people doing? How do you think the people feel when they're doing these jobs? Which job would you prefer? Why? Make notes in English and talk for about three minutes.*

b) *Prepare answers to the following questions, so that you can speak freely and confidently. Talk for about three minutes. You can record your speech.*

- Why do you think work experience is important for young people?
- Do you have a weekend job or an after-school job?
- Talk about any work experience that you have. What did you like about it and what didn't you like?
- What would you like to do when you leave school? Go to university? Spend time abroad? Train for a job?

7 MEDIATION　Small ads

MEDIATION

You have met an American student. She doesn't know much German but would like to have a job for a few hours a day. You find some suitable jobs in the local newspaper. Make notes in English first so that you can tell her about the jobs. Use your exercise book for your notes.

1　**Café am Brunnen**

Aushilfe gesucht für ca. 3 Stunden vorm. od. nachm.
Arbeiten in Küche und Café (z. B. Gemüse putzen, Küche aufräumen, Tische decken u. abräumen). Servieren von Eis und Kuchen im Gastgarten.
Gute Bezahlung.
Tel.: 793 501

2　**Hotel am Domplatz**

Für die Rezeption suchen wir **ab sofort** eine Kraft mit sehr guten **Englischkenntnissen**.
Aufgaben: telefonische Auskunft u. Betreuung ausländischer Gäste. Erfahrung in der Hotelbranche erwünscht, aber nicht Voraussetzung. Halbtags od. stundenweise als Aushilfe.
Überdurchschnittliche Bezahlung.
Tel.: 482 502 (Fr. Lenz)

3　**Englischsprachige Kinderbetreuung**

für amerikanische Familie gesucht
(Kinder 2 und 4 J.).
Mo–Fr, 13–17 Uhr. Keine Arbeit im Haushalt.
Führerschein nicht erforderlich.
Tel.: 602 335

4　Student/in für **englische Konversation** gesucht.
Mo u. Do vorm. je 2 St. (Gruppe: 6 Pers.),
2. Gruppe Di u. Fr möglich, **native speaker** willkommen! Deutschkenntnisse nicht erforderlich. Tel.: 496 395 (Vera)

Well, there's a job in a café. You have to …

How did you do?

Check your answers to the exercises on p. 88. Then answer the questions below with Yes or No.
If you tick No or would like some extra practice on that point, go to the exercise in your workbook
(▸ pp. 54–76).

	Yes	No	Exercise

1 LISTENING First day at work

1 Hast du dir beim 1. Hören Notizen gemacht (z.B. Zahlen, Farben)? ▸ 3, 5

2 Konntest du den amerikanischen Akzent mühelos verstehen? ▸ 6, 7, 9

3 Hast du dem Sprechtempo problemlos folgen können? ▸ 8, 9

2 READING Jobs

1 Konntest du schnell herausfinden, um was es in den Texten geht? ▸ 10, 16a

2 Konntest du Antworten auf die Detailfragen problemlos finden? ▸ 11–13

3 Hast du die Bedeutung unbekannter Wörter erschließen können? ▸ 15, 16b

3 WRITING A formal letter

1 Hast du auf eine geeignete Form geachtet (z.B. *addresses, date*)? ▸ 21b

2 Hast du eine passende Gruß- und Schlussformel benutzt? ▸ 21a

3 Hast du deine Fragen (direkt und indirekt) mühelos bilden können? ▸ 23, 36

4 Hast du deine Rechtschreibung/Grammatik überprüft und deine Fehler korrigiert? ▸ 37, 38

4 WRITING Your CV

1 Hast du alle erforderlichen Informationen in einer passenden Reihenfolge präsentiert? ▸ 22a+c

2 Hast du ein kurzes *personal statement* geschrieben? ▸ 22b

3 Hast du deine Rechtschreibung/Grammatik überprüft und deine Fehler korrigiert? ▸ 37, 38

5 WRITING An informal letter

1 Hast du eine passende Gruß- und Schlussformel benutzt? ▸ 20

2 Hast du deinem Text eine Struktur gegeben? ▸ 20

6 SPEAKING Jobs and work experience

1 Hast du mit dem *present progressive* beschrieben, was die Personen gerade machen? ▸ 29

2 Hast du mit passenden Adjektiven die Jobs beschrieben? ▸ 35

3 Hast du die erforderlichen Vokabeln für die Bildbeschreibung gewusst? ▸ 24a, 35

4 Konntest du drei Minuten zusammenhängend sprechen? ▸ 24b, 25b

7 MEDIATION Small ads

1 Hast du beachtet, mit eigenen Worten nur das Wesentliche weiterzugeben bzw. nicht alles wörtlich zu übersetzen? ▸ 26, 27

2 Hast du (falls nötig) für unbekannte Wörter Umschreibungen benutzt (*paraphrasing*)? ▸ 34

3 Hast du modale Hilfsverben richtig benutzt (*can, have to, needn't* usw.)? ▸ 28

Unit 3 Stand up for your rights

1 Human rights ▶ pp. 50–51

a) Name four more of the rights that are set down in the Universal Declaration of Human Rights.

the right to freedom from discrimination, the right to freedom of religion, the right to freedom of

speech, the right to choose your government/vote, the right to education

b) Give a few examples of racial discrimination in history. Make notes.

Native Americans, slave trade, African–Americans, Aborigines in Australia, apartheid in South Africa

c) What other main kinds of discrimination can you think of? Name them.

colour, age, religion, nationality, against women

d) Which right is the most important one for you? Explain why.

2 READING WORKING WITH THE TEXT First Amendment ▶ pp. 52–53 • WB (pp. 77–78)

Read pp. 52–53 of your student's book again and answer the questions in a few sentences each. Write in your exercise book.

a) How would you assess Mr Neck's History lesson on a scale of 1 (very bad) to 5 (very good)? Explain your assessment. Think about the meaning of 'free speech' and look for lines in the text which support your views.

b) What kind of person is David Petrakis? Look at what Melinda, the narrator, says about him and what you learn about him from his words and actions.

c) Find the meaning of 'suck-ups' (l. 49) in a dictionary. In Melinda's opinion, who are the 'suck-ups' in the class and why?

d) What is your opinion about ll. 62–69?

e) How do you think the situation between Mr Neck, the students of the 8th grade History class and David Petrakis might develop? How could the lesson continue? How might the next History lesson be?

f) Does this chapter make you want to read the whole novel 'Speak'? Say why or why not.

WB, pp. 58–62

3 REVISION Freedom of speech (Passive verb forms) ▶ p. 55 • GF (pp. 161–163)

Complete the text with passive forms of the verbs in brackets. Be careful with the tenses.

Speakers' Corner in Hyde Park __is visited__ (visit) by tourists

from all over the world. It __is thought of__ (think of) as a

powerful symbol of the freedom of speech, a place where

everyone has the right to listen and to be heard.

The north-east corner of Hyde Park __has been used__

(use) as a place for public protest for over a century and a half.

It started in 1855 when meetings and protests __were held__ (hold) there by working people wanting

democratic reforms. Since 1872 Speakers' Corner __has been recognized__ (recognize) officially as a

place for public speaking. People __are allowed__ (allow) to speak on almost any topic without fear of

the law. Only two things __are not allowed__ (not allow): speaking against the Royal Family and

wanting to overthrow[1] the British government.

3503

4 REVISION Nelson Mandela (Participle clauses instead of relative clauses) ▶ p. 56 • WB (p. 85)

a) Improve the style of the article on Nelson Mandela by using participle clauses instead of relative clauses.

Nelson Mandela was the symbol of the fight against apartheid, the South African system which separated people by race.

separating

Mandela was born in 1918. He studied law[2] and in 1952 opened the first law firm in South Africa which was owned by blacks.

owned

He had joined the African National Congress (ANC), an organization which fought for the freedom of black people in South Africa. He soon became an ANC leader and in 1964 was sent to prison for life because of his protest activities.

fighting

In the 1980s a campaign[3] that was supported by people in South Africa and around the world to free Mandela grew. Under President F.W. de Klerk, the government set Mandela free in 1990.

supported

Mandela became president of the ANC in 1991. He and de Klerk then worked together to end apartheid. They wanted to change South Africa into a democracy that gave people of all colours equal rights. In 1993 they won the Nobel Peace[4] Prize for their work. In 1994 South Africa had its first free elections which resulted[5] in Mandela becoming the country's first black president. He retired[6] from active politics in 1999.

giving

resulting

3504

b) Find out more about apartheid. What did it mean for black people? Write a paragraph. Use participle clauses where possible to improve your style.

[1] overthrow [ˌəʊvəˈθrəʊ] *stürzen* [2] law [lɔː] *Rechtswissenschaft, Gesetz* [3] campaign [kæmˈpeɪn] *Kampagne*
[4] peace [piːs] *Frieden* [5] result in [rɪˈzʌlt] *führen zu* [6] retire [rɪˈtaɪə] *sich zurückziehen*

5 I heard a man shouting (Verbs of perception + object + present participle) ▶ p. 56 • WB (p. 85)

Salim saw Speakers' Corner for the first time. Later he told a friend what he had seen and heard people doing.
Complete the sentences with the words given.

1 (about fifty people – stand):

I saw *about fifty people standing* round a man in a funny hat with the British flag on it.

2 (the man – shout): I heard *the man shouting* something about the government.

3 (the crowd – cheer – clap): A bit later I heard *the crowd cheering and clapping* .

4 (another man – wave – sing): A bit further[1] away I saw *another man waving*

his arms and *singing* .

5 (policeman – watch): I also saw *a policeman watching* the crowd.

6 (some kids – laugh): I heard *some kids laughing* at the man who was singing.

3605 7 (lots of tourists – take): I saw *lots of tourists taking* photos too.

6 The man from Atlanta (Participle clauses instead of adverbial clauses) ▶ p. 57 • WB (p. 86)

This is part of a student's essay on Martin Luther King's early life. Improve the style by using participle clauses instead of the underlined parts. Rewrite these adverbial clauses with participle clauses.

1 Even as a young boy, Martin Luther King was good at speaking in public. <u>Because he had won a prize</u> for one of his speeches, he had to go to Washington with his teacher for the awards ceremony.
2 <u>When he was sitting in the bus</u> on the way back to Atlanta, King was told by the driver to give his seat to a white man. He did not see why he should, but <u>because he did not want to make problems</u> for his teacher, he did what the driver said.
3 <u>As they were discriminated because of their skin colour,</u> black Americans had a difficult life.
4 <u>Because he had experienced discrimination as a child,</u> King knew how black people in the South felt.
5 <u>When King was studying to become a minister in the North,</u> he saw that black and white people could live together in peace as friends. So why should it not be possible in the South?
6 Later, <u>when he had studied the teachings of Gandhi about non-violent protest,</u> King hoped that segregation in the South could be ended without violence.
7 <u>Because he wanted to change things,</u> King became a civil rights activist.

1 *Having won a prize ...*

2 *Sitting in the bus ..., ... not wanting to make problems ...*

3 *Discriminated because of their skin colour, ...*

4 *Having experienced discrimination as a child, ...*

5 *Studying to become a minister in the North, ...*

6 *..., having studied the teachings of Gandhi ..., ...*

3606 7 *Wanting to change things, ...*

[1] further ['fɜːðə] *weiter*

7 WORLDS (Compound participles) ▶ p. 58

a) *Match and write words to make compound adjectives.*

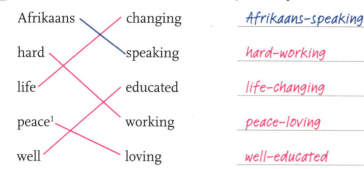

Afrikaans	changing	*Afrikaans-speaking*
hard	speaking	*hard-working*
life	educated	*life-changing*
peace[1]	working	*peace-loving*
well	loving	*well-educated*

> **INFO BOX**
>
> Nelson Mandela was in prison on Robben Island off the coast of Cape Town from 1964 to 1990. His prison number was 46664 (four, double six, six, four), which meant that he was the 466th prisoner on the island in 1964. Today people still talk about Nelson Mandela as 'prisoner 46664'.
> The former prison, often called the Alcatraz of South Africa, is now a museum and a tourist attraction.

b) *Rewrite the sentences. Replace the underlined sentence parts with adjectives from a).*

1 During apartheid a <u>white minority who spoke Afrikaans</u> ruled[2] South Africa.

During apartheid an Afrikaans-speaking white minority ruled South Africa.

2 <u>Blacks who worked hard</u> could not enjoy the comfortable lifestyle of whites.

Hard-working blacks could not enjoy the comfortable lifestyle of whites.

3 In South Africa it was very difficult for a black person to become a <u>lawyer[3] with a good education</u>.

In South Africa it was very difficult for a black person to become a well-educated lawyer.

4 After almost 30 years in prison, Nelson Mandela was still a <u>man who loved peace</u>.

3707

After almost 30 years in prison, Nelson Mandela was still a peace-loving man.

8 The bus boycott (Participle clauses giving additional information) ▶ p. 58 • WB (p. 86)

Improve the written style by making one sentence out of two.

1 King and his followers led a bus boycott in Montgomery. They wanted to take action against segregation.
King and his followers led a bus boycott in Montgomery, wanting to take action against segregation.

2 They asked black people not to use the buses. They hoped the action would force the bus company to end segregation.

They asked black people not to use the buses, hoping the action would force the bus company to end segregation.

3 King was worried about the effects of the boycott. He thought it may make the daily lives of black people even more difficult.

King was worried about the effects of the boycott, thinking it may make the daily lives of black people even more difficult.

4 But the bus boycott ended successfully and it made King's name known throughout America.

But the bus boycott ended successfully, making King's name known throughout America.

3708

[1] peace [piːs] *Frieden* [2] rule [ruːl] *regieren* [3] lawyer ['lɔːjə] *Anwalt/Anwältin*

9 Extra **A dream of freedom**   (Participle clauses with conjunctions)   ▶ *p. 58 • WB (p. 86)*

Sometimes a conjunction is necessary to make the meaning of a participle clause clear. Rewrite the sentences about Ellis Island using a participle clause with a conjunction.

1 While you are visiting New York, you will most probably go to Ellis Island.
  While visiting New York, you will most probably go to Ellis Island.

2 Before they entered the USA, immigrants had to pass a medical inspection[1].

  Before entering the USA, immigrants had to pass a medical inspection.

3 If they were diagnosed[2] with an eye disease, immigrants were sent back.

  If diagnosed with an eye disease, immigrants were sent back.

4 After they had passed the medical and the legal inspection, about 98% of all immigrants were allowed into the country.

  After having passed the medical and the legal inspection, about 98% of all immigrants were allowed

  into the country.

5 Although babies were born on Ellis Island, they did not automatically become American citizens.

  Although (being) born on Ellis Island, babies did not automatically become American citizens.

3809

10 WORDS   Politics   ▶ *p. 62*

Use suitable words from the box to complete the sentences below.

> aims • budget • campaign • citizens • council • debate • democracy • elect • election
> government • mayor • members of parliament • minister • opposition • parliament
> party members • pass laws • political party • politician • politics • power • president
> proposal • reforms • represent • run/stand for office • supporters • term of office • *vote*

1 In a democracy, an important human right is the right to *vote* . You also have the right to

  run/stand for office   .

2 In the UK there is a general (national) *election*   every four or five years, and there are local

  elections too. British *citizens*   who are over 18 years of age can *elect*   a candidate

  to represent their area in parliament.

3 The US president is elected for a four-year *term of office*   . He can only be elected twice.

4 In Roland, Iowa, Sam Juhl was elected *mayor*   at the age of only 18. The other

  members of the City *Council*   were all older than him.

5 My brother knows a lot about *politics*   . I think he would make a good *politician*   .

3810

  Maybe he will join a *political party*   and live at 10 Downing Street one day!

[1] medical inspection ['medɪkl ɪn'spekʃn] *medizinische Untersuchung*   [2] diagnose ['daɪəgnəʊz] *diagnostizieren*

11 EVERYDAY ENGLISH   SPEAKING Talking about politics   ▸ p. 62 • WB (p. 79)

You have an English friend who will be a first-time voter at the next general election. You'd like to ask her some questions. Write them in English.

1 Welche Partei sie unterstützt: *Which (political) party do you support?*

2 Welche Bildungspolitik ihre Partei vertritt: *What's their policy on education?*

3 Ob sie planen, mehr Geld für die Bildung auszugeben: *Are they planning to/Are they going to spend more money on education?*

4 Welche Änderungen im Schulwesen (*educational system*) ihre Partei plant: *Which changes are they planning to make/are they going to make to the educational system?*

5 Ob sie vorhat zu wählen: *Are you going to vote?*

6 Ob sie es für eine gute Idee halten würde, Oberstufenschülern (*sixth-form students*) mehr Rechte zu geben:

Do you think it would be a good idea to give sixth-form students more rights?

WB, pp. 68–69

12 MEDIATION   Demonstrating   ▸ p. 63 • WB (p. 79)

You see people demonstrating. Explain to an English friend what the people are protesting against? What do they want the government/people to do? If you don't know a word, paraphrase it.

You: *Well, they are protesting against different things. One poster says 'NO' to …*

'B, pp.)–71

¹ stem cell research ['stem sel]   ² nuclear power [ˌnjuːklɪə 'pauə]

13 READING   Voting rights in the UK   ▶ p. 64 • WB (pp. 77–78)

a) *Read the text about Emmeline Pankhurst, who fought for women's suffrage[1] in Britain. Then find suitable headings for the paragraphs. Write a letter A–F in the box. There is one more heading than you need.*

A	A supportive husband	B	Failure	C	A militant course
D	Victory	E	Slow beginnings	F	Family background

E In Britain at the start of the 19th century only rich men were allowed to vote. People who were not rich also wanted political rights, but Parliament refused to allow reforms. As a result, the people's anger[2] grew and riots broke out all over the country. Thousands demonstrated on the streets. Some were killed. Finally, in 1832 Parliament was forced to pass a law allowing more men to vote. Votes for women were still unthinkable.

F Even at the start of the 20th century women still did not have the vote. Some protested peacefully, but nothing changed. A woman called Emmeline Goulden, born in Manchester in 1858, also believed that women should have voting rights. Her mother was a feminist and her father, a successful businessman, had strong political views. As a teenager in the 1870s Emmeline went to women's suffrage meetings with her mother. Emmeline was clever. She loved reading, but because she was a girl, she did not receive the same education as her five brothers. A boy's education was thought to be more important.

A When Emmeline was 20, she married Dr Richard Pankhurst, a lawyer[3] and a socialist who was 24 years older than her. He was a strong supporter of voting rights for women. Emmeline and her husband worked together on social projects, trying to improve the lives of the poor. They had five children in ten years, but Emmeline never stopped working. Emmeline's husband became ill and died in 1898. She was left alone with her children, but she continued to work hard to help poor women living in terrible conditions[4] in workhouses, especially teenage mothers.

C In 1903 she founded the Women's Social and Political Union, together with her oldest daughter Christabel, who was studying to become a lawyer. After a few years, having realized that peaceful protest came to nothing, these women took up the fight for women's rights in a radical way. They disturbed[5] meetings in Parliament, they encouraged women to break the law by attacking police officers, breaking windows, setting fire to buildings, anything in order to get the attention[6] of both the public and the law-makers in Parliament. They became known as 'suffragettes'. Emmeline led protest marches and held speeches in the USA. In Britain Emmeline and Christabel were arrested and put in prison many times. Many other members of the WSPU were arrested too. Some went on hunger strike in prison, but were force-fed. Emmeline became seriously ill. In 1912 Christabel escaped to Paris, where she was able to organize further political campaigns[7] without fear of being arrested.

D When the First World War started in 1914, women still did not have the vote. However, Emmeline stopped all militant activities and wanted women to support the government and work for their country. Many women did the work of men who were fighting in the war. When the war was over in 1918, women in Britain over the age of 30 and all men over the age of 21 were given voting rights. Ten years later in 1928 – all women were given the same full voting rights as men – in the same year as Emmeline Pankhurst's death.

WB, pp.
58–62

b) *In your exercise book, write a timeline of important events in Emmeline Pankhurst's life.*

◉ **c)** *Explain the important role Emmeline Pankhurst had in getting voting rights for women. Do you agree with her methods? Write two paragraphs in your exercise book.*

[1] suffrage ['sʌfrɪdʒ] *Wahlrecht* [2] anger ['æŋgə] *Wut* [3] lawyer ['lɔːjə] *Anwalt/Anwältin* [4] condition [kən'dɪʃn] *Zustand* [5] disturb [dɪ'stɜːb] *stören* [6] attention [ə'tenʃn] *Aufmerksamkeit* [7] campaign [kæm'peɪn] *Kampagne*

14 LISTENING   Discussion about voting   ▶ p. 64 • WB (p. 77) 🎧 12

a) *Listen to the four students' discussion about voting. Then mark the correct answers.*

1 The students talk about…

- election promises. ☐
- the voting system in the USA. ☐
- why it's important to use your right to vote. ✔

2 Which students think voting is very important?

- The two girls. ☐
- One boy and one girl. ✔
- Just one girl. ☐

b) *Now listen again for details. While you are listening, note dates or names. Are the statements true or false? Write T or F.*

1 Fran's sister is going to vote at the next election.	F
2 Tom thinks that politicians make promises but they don't keep them.	T
3 Mel believes that every vote counts.	T
4 Syed thinks it's stupid to complain about how the country is run if you don't vote.	T
5 Mel tells the other students about the history of women's votes in the UK.	T
6 Tom thinks everyone should get involved with politics and voting.	F
7 The first country to give women the vote was New Zealand.	T
8 In Germany and Ireland women got the vote in the same year.	F
9 In the UK women got full voting rights in 1928.	T
10 In 1980 women in Switzerland got the same voting rights as men.	F

WB, pp. 54–57

15 WRITING   The right to strike   ▶ p. 64 • WB (pp. 81–82)

Read what a spokesman[1] of the postal[2] workers' union[3] and some postal workers said at a strike meeting. Mark the facts, not opinions. Then use the facts to write a short report, making suitable changes in sentence structure. Write in your exercise book.

The union has decided that postal workers will go on strike from Monday next week. There'll be a series of one-day strikes in different parts of the UK. The reason is that we think we are not being treated[4] fairly by the management. There have been disagreements about pay, job cuts and changes to working conditions[5] for a long time, but nothing happens. It's all just talk. Although there's less mail than there used to be, there's more work to do than ever before, but not more money. We're also afraid that our jobs are not safe.

Over 20,000 postal workers will be involved in England and Scotland, more than half of us in London, the rest in cities such as Bristol, Manchester, Edinburgh and Liverpool. Other cities will follow, I expect. We think it could be very serious because people are angry. A strike across Britain would involve about 160,000 workers. I imagine it would cost the country millions. And there will be public protests.

The action could lead to a nationwide postal strike in winter if the union doesn't come to an agreement with the management. But we have to strike. If workers up and down the country don't take a stand[6], the employers will never improve things for us. One thing is clear, this strike action will be the most serious for over three years.

WB, pp. 63–67

From Monday next week postal workers in the UK will go on strike. There will be a series of one-day strikes involving over 20,000 postal workers in England and Scotland …

[1] spokesman ['spəʊksmən] *Sprecher*   [2] postal ['pəʊstl] *Post-, postalisch*   [3] union ['juːnɪən] *Gewerkschaft*   [4] treat [triːt] *behandeln*   [5] condition [kən'dɪʃn] *Bedingung*   [6] take a stand *Stellung beziehen*

16 SPEAKING COURSE Part 3:   Oral summary   ▶ p. 65 • WB (p. 81)

a) *How do you give a good oral summary? Tick the correct boxes.*

You should include your personal opinion.	☐	Explain the general situation (5 Ws) first. ✔
Use the present tense. ✔		Give only the main action, events or ideas. ✔
Give relevant facts only, without description. ✔		Include lots of details. ☐

b) *Nina tells a friend about the film 'Blood Diamond'. It is not a good oral summary. First, mark the sentences or sentence parts that you can improve or leave out. Then rewrite the summary, making any necessary changes.*

I saw this film 'Blood Diamond' with my brother last night on TV. It was on quite late, but we had a pizza while we were watching it. It's about the civil war in Sierra Leone, about 1999, my brother said. Well, anyway … erm…, there's lots of fighting between government soldiers and the RUF[1] rebels[2]. The pizza was cool, by the way. The rebels force men to work in the diamond fields, and they take kids from their families and force them to become child soldiers. Well, there's this nice guy, black guy, called Solomon whose family is kidnapped when the rebels attack his village. He's forced to work in the diamond fields and his young son becomes a child soldier, and … well, it's pretty hard stuff. It really plays on your emotions[3]. Anyway, Solomon finds this huge diamond and hides it. Leo DiCaprio plays Danny Archer, a white guy from Zimbabwe who wants the diamond – same as everybody else – but in the end after a lot of confusing stuff he helps the black guy to get back his family in exchange for the diamond. Oh, and there's this American woman too. She's a kind of journalist. Well, she helps Archer and Solomon and she publishes the whole story of the dirty diamond trade in her magazine. So this is good, I guess. The film shows how children's rights are violated[4]. This made me angry because it really happens in lots of countries, so my brother says. It also shows how terrible civil war is, when people fighting for power stop at nothing. My brother likes fast-moving action, so he liked the film, but it made me sad.

c) **Extra** *Summarize the main points of a TV programme for someone who didn't see it. Choose, for example, a crime drama, a documentary or an episode of a soap opera. Make notes first and be prepared to give your four-minute oral summary in class. Remember to use the present tense. Write in your exercise book.*

WB, pp. 68–69

---

[1] RUF = Revolutionary United Front   [2] rebel ['rebl] *Rebell/in*   [3] emotion [ɪ'məʊʃn] *Gefühl*   [4] violate ['vaɪəleɪt] *verletzen, verstoßen gegen*

17 Extra **Background File:** **Why are the British such a mixture?** ▶ pp. 67–68

a) Read pp. 67–68 in your student's book again. Choose the correct answer: A, B or C.

1 Who lived in Britain 2000 years ago?

| A̶ Celts, Picts and Silures. | B Vikings. | C Angles, Saxons and Jutes. |

2 How long did the Romans stay in Britan?

| A About 700 years. | B About 370 years. | C̶ About 400 years. |

3 Where did William the Conqueror come from?

| A Denmark. | B Norway. | C̶ France. |

4 In which century did the British start to found colonies in North America?

| A 16th. | B̶ 17th. | C 18th. |

5 When did India become independent from Britain?

| A In 1776. | B̶ In 1947. | C In 1960. |

b) Write in a few sentences what each part (1–5) of the text on pp. 67–68 in your student's book is about.
   *Part **1** describes/explains/deals with/gives information about…*

Part 1 explains that in the early history of Britain many different tribes lived in the country, including the Romans in 43 AD, the Anglo-Saxons in the 6th century, the Vikings in the 9th century and the Normans in 1066. Part 2 describes how from about 1600 Britain founded colonies in North America and became rich by slave-trading. In 1776 these colonies became independent. Part 3 deals with Britain's control over India from the 18th century. It describes how the British East India Company and the British Empire under Queen Victoria made England rich and powerful. Part 4 explains that in the 20th century many countries under British control became independent, and that many Commonwealth citizens from India, Pakistan and Jamaica came to work in Britain and settled there. Part 5 describes how EU citizens from Eastern Europe and asylum seekers from Nigeria and Somalia have moved into Britain in recent years. Also, Britain still has strong links to the USA and to former Commonwealth countries.

18 WORDS **Prepositions** ▶ p. 69

Choose and underline the correct preposition.

After laws (against/for/of) race discrimination were made in the 1960s, the situation (about/from/of) black people in Britain began to improve, but (in/on/at) the whole white people still have better chances (in/for/of) life than blacks. In the 21st century thousands of immigrants (out of/of/from) East European countries have moved (to/into/in) Britain. Although Britain is now more multicultural than ever before, it still has strong links (with/to/in) its former Commonwealth countries.

Unit 4 Teen world

1 Typical teens ▶ pp. 78–79

Look at pp. 78–79 of your student's book again. Then answer the questions in note form. Use your notes for a discussion in class.

1 Which aspects of teen life do the photos show?

free time, friendships, jobs, love, problems, …

2 Would you say that the photos give a typical picture of teens? Why or why not?

Yes/No, I think the photos

3 Write down other important aspects of teen life that are not shown in the photos.

school, sports, family life, …

4 What message does the cartoon on p. 79 of your student's book want to give its readers? Explain.

I think the message of the cartoon is that

2 SPEAKING Teens and their mobiles ▶ p. 81 • WB (p. 79) 🎧 13

INFO BOX

In Germany 92% of young people aged 12 to 19 have a mobile phone, 69% of kids from 10 to 13, 16% of kids under 10!
Half of the kids pay part of their monthly mobile bill[1]. 20% of the kids pay the bill themselves!
(Source: KidsVA 2009, Egmont Ehapa Verlag)

Listen to what six British students say about how they use their mobile phones. In the pauses, give your opinion on what each student says. Use phrases such as:

- I agree with … (completely).
- I don't agree with …
- I can't understand why …
- I think … is right/wrong.
- I think it's stupid to say …

- In my opinion, …
- I don't think it's fair to …
- It's a good idea to … because …

1 Emma:

WB, pp. 68–69

🖥 4402

This is how you might give your opinion on what Emma says:
I agree with Emma's parents. In my opinion, Emma is unfair. Why should her parents pay so much money just for her fun? I think that a lot of Emma's phone calls and messages are probably unnecessary anyway. If I was her mum or dad, I woudn't pay her bills …

[1] bill [bɪl] *Rechnung*

3 STUDY SKILLS   Argumentative writing   ▶ *p. 82 • SF (p. 147)*

Discuss the following topic:

> Parents should not allow school students to have a TV in their room.

Add arguments and points to the following outline or use your own ideas. Write your complete text in your exercise book or on the computer.

1	Introduction	Lots of school students watch TV in their free time, but should parents allow them to have a TV in their room? …
2	First point of view	Parents allow their children to have their own TV mostly for practical reasons.
2.1	First argument	First, young people don't always want to see the same programmes …
2.2	Second argument	…
2.3	…	…
3	Opposite point of view	However, is it really a good idea for school students to watch TV when …
3.1	First argument	Young people maybe watch programmes that are …
3.2	Second argument	Another argument is that …
3.3	…	…
4	Conclusion	After looking at both sides, I think that …
4.1	Summing up	To sum up, in my opinion … because there are more disadvantages than advantages for having …
4.2	Personal opinion	That's why I …

WB, pp. 63–67

4 REVISION   What did they say? (Indirect speech)   ▶ *p. 83 • GF (pp. 170–171)*

Report the conversation with: **say, tell, reply, want to know**.

1 Are you going to the party on Saturday?

3 But Darren asked me to go with him!

5 What are you going to tell him?

2 Yes, I think I'm going with Darren.

4 Really? I can't believe it!

6 I'll tell him I'm going with his best friend. He won't like that.

1 Joy asked Shazia _if she was going to the party on Saturday._

2 Shazia said that she thought _she was going with Darren._

3 Joy _told Shazia that Darren had asked her to go with him._

4 Shazia _replied that she couldn't believe it._

5 _Joy wanted to know what Shazia was going to tell Darren._

4504   6 _Shazia said she would tell him that she was going with his best friend. He wouldn't like that._

5 **EVERYDAY ENGLISH** **Asking someone out** ▶ *p. 83*

Write a dialogue in your exercise book. The phrases below may help you.

1 Oh, hi! I was wondering if you'd like to …

2 Well, I'm not sure whether I …

- Well, how about …?
- Have you got any plans for …?
- Shall I pick you up?

- I don't really fancy going …
- I think I'd prefer …
- That would be great. Thanks!

6 WORDS Teens in trouble ▶ *p. 85*

a) *Choose words from the box in the correct form to complete the sentences.*

> attack · ban · behaviour · cause · court · fights · kick · law · motorbikes
> offer · order · organization · police · punishment · straighten up · vandalize

1 The 'B' in 'ASBO' means __behaviour__ .

2 The 'O' in 'ASBO' means __order__ .

3 Shane was given a four-yer ASBO by the

__court__ .

4 He __caused__ serious trouble many times.

5 He __kicked__ footballs against houses and cars.

6 He rode __motorbikes__ on the pavement.

7 He __attacked__ other teenagers.

8 He was __banned__ from some areas of town.

9 The ASBO was his __punishment__ .

10 It helped him to __straighten up__ his life.

b) *Shane is now 17 and doing well. How do you think he feels about himself and about his future?*

4606 Ideas: *feels proud of himself · serious about work · looking forward to his future · job and money*

Now you

Do you think that an ASBO is a good way to stop anti-social behaviour? Write a formal letter to a magazine and give reasons for your opinion. Read pp. 84–85 of your student's book again first. Use your exercise book or a computer.

Ideas: *have nothing to do · no job · no money · feel bored and angry · don't care · need 'fun'*

> *Dear Sir or Madam*
>
> *I would like to share my opinion on anti-social behaviour and teenagers with readers of your magazine.*
>
> *First, …*
>
> *Second, …*

7 SPEAKING COURSE Part 4:
Talking about ASBOs (Having a discussion) ▶ *p. 86* • *WB (p. 80)* 🎧 **14, 15**

Choose and tick the correct phrase. During a discussion, what would you say …

1 … when you want to know someone's opinion?

> ☐ A I see what you mean.   ☑ B What do you think?
>
> ☐ C Could you say that again, please?

2 … when you say what you think?

> ☐ A I agree with you.   ☑ B In my opinion, …   ☐ C No, that's not right.

3 … when you think/feel the same as the speaker?

> ☐ A Could you say that again? ☐ B Let me explain.   ☑ C I agree with you.

4 … when you want to say that you understand the speaker's point?

> ☑ A I see what you mean.   ☐ B Wait a minute. Let me finish.
>
> ☐ C Sorry, I don't agree with you.

5 … when you are speaking and someone else starts to speak?

> ☐ A No, that's not right.   ☐ B Could you say that again, please?
>
> ☑ C Wait a minute. Let me finish.

6 … when you don't think/feel the same as the speaker?

> ☑ A Sorry, I don't agree with you.   ☐ B I know you're right.   ☐ C That's true.

7 … when you think what someone said is wrong?

> ☐ A I don't understand what you mean. ☑ B No, that's not right. ☐ C You're right.

b) *Read the discussion phrases below. Then listen (🎧 14) to Guy, Mel and Ali, three UK teenagers who are talking about ASBOs. Write down the order that you hear the discussion phrases in (2–11).*

I agree with you.	5	That's a good point.	3
In my opinion, …	1	I see what you mean.	9
Wait a minute. Let me finish.	2	Sorry, but I don't agree with you.	6
What do you think?	4	No, that's not right.	10
First, …	7	That's true.	11
Second, …	8		

c) *Listen again (🎧 15) to the discussion and in the pauses fill in the missing phrases from b). Do this exercise at least twice.*

> That's a good point.
> I see what you mean.
> But I don't agree with you.
> In my opinion, …

WB, pp.
8–69

4707
4708

8 REVISION What do they mean? (Modal verbs) ▶ p. 87 • WB (p. 83)

In national parks you often see signs like these. What do they mean? Tick all the correct answers below.

Test

1	PLEASE DO NOT FEED THE ANIMALS

2	Keep gate¹ closed at all times

4	Please keep dogs under control

5	

1 You mustn't feed the animals. ✔
 You needn't feed the animals. ☐
 You are not allowed to feed the animals. ✔
 You shouldn't feed the animals. ✔

2 You have to keep the gate closed. ✔
 You must keep the gate closed. ✔
 You needn't close the gate. ☐
 You mustn't leave² the gate open. ✔

3 You aren't allowed to pick flowers. ✔
 You don't have to pick flowers. ☐
 You mustn't pick flowers. ✔
 You can pick flowers. ☐

4808

4 You have to keep your dog under control. ✔
 You must let your dog run free. ☐
 You mustn't let your dog run free. ✔
 You must keep your dog under control. ✔

5 You can camp here. ✔
 You are allowed to camp here. ✔
 You don't have to camp here. ☐
 You must camp here. ☐

6 You mustn't make a fire here. ✔
 You have to make a fire here. ☐
 You needn't make a fire here. ☐
 You are not allowed to make a fire here. ✔

9 Blue box: Translating German 'sollen' (should, had better and be supposed to) ▶ p. 87, p. 207

a) *Choose the correct form:* should/shouldn't, had better (not), be (not) supposed to.

1 ASBOs _are supposed to_ punish young troublemakers. But are they really effective?

2 Shane's former friend has got an ASBO too. He _had better not_ break the rules, or he may

 have to go to prison. For example, he _isn't supposed to_ go out at night, so he _had better/_

 should learn to spend his evenings at home.

3 Teenagers who go to boot camp _are supposed to_ learn discipline, but do they learn to make

 decisions about what's right or wrong themselves?

4 _Should_ people at boot camp be treated so badly? They _shouldn't_ be punished without
 reason.

b) *Write what you are supposed to do and not supposed to do at home and at school. Use your exercise book and write at least three sentences for each place.*

I'm supposed to keep my room tidy. I'm not supposed to watch TV before I've done my homework.

¹ gate [geɪt] *Tor* ² leave *hier: lassen*

10 Blue box: People needing help (the + adjective) ▸ p. 91, p. 209

Complete the sentences with phrases like the poor, poor people, the poor man/woman.

1 Do you think the government does enough for _the poor/poor people_ (poor)?

2 _The blind man_ (blind) living near us is called Mr Wilson. He has a lovely dog.

3 Our youth club is collecting money for a mini-bus for _the disabled/disabled people_ (disabled).

4 _The disabled woman_ (disabled) who works with my mum used to be good at athletics before her accident.

5 I met _an unemployed man/woman_ (unemployed[1]) who has been looking for work for three years.

6 I wonder how much money _the rich/rich people_ (rich) donate to charities.

11 REVISION Volunteering (Adverbs or adjectives after certain verbs) ▸ p. 91

On his return from India, Ed, a young American volunteer, talked about his trip. Use the adjective or adverb form of the word in brackets.

'I went to India because the volunteer project in a village near Pune sounded _exciting_ (exciting) – and it was. We repaired a small school building, painted it and planted trees. We got on _well_ (good) with the local people and they seemed _happy_ (happy) to have us there. We felt really _useful_ (useful). Every day the camp leaders looked _carefully_ (careful) at our work and were pleased with what we had achieved. The school looked pretty _good_ (good) when we left. I'll miss the friendly people and the Indian food, which smelled and tasted _delicious_ (delicious). I would go back there _gladly_ (glad) and help again. Maybe next year.'

4911
4912

12 Translating German adverbs (English verbs instead of German adverbs) ▸ p. 91

Match the German adverbs to the English verbs. Then use some of them to translate the sentence parts below.

anscheinend — used to
früher — seem to
gern/ungern — I hope
hoffentlich — like/don't like

immer wieder — keep on (doing)
lieber — happen to
vermutlich — prefer to
zufällig — I suppose

1 Hoffentlich werde ich die Chance haben, eines Tages an einem Hilfsprojekt teilzunehmen.

I hope I'll have the opportunity/chance to do volunteer work one day.

2 Mein Vater hat früher als Freiwilliger (*volunteer*) in Afrika gearbeitet,

My father used to work as a volunteer/do volunteer work in Africa.

3 Ich würde lieber bei einem europäischen Programm mitmachen. Ich würde gern in Russland arbeiten.

4913

I would prefer to join a European programme. _I'd like to work_ in Russia.

[1] unemployed [ˌʌnɪmˈplɔɪd] *arbeitslos*

13 They make you work hard (let/make somebody do something) ▶ p. 92

a) *Underline the correct form in the brackets.*

1 Teenagers volunteer to go to boot camp instead of prison. Nobody (<u>makes</u>/lets) them go.

2 At boot camp they (<u>make</u>/let) you work really hard.

3 They (<u>don't let</u>/don't make) you go home until the six months are over.

4 They (don't make/<u>don't let</u>) you have any contact with family or friends, not even a phone call.

5 The instructors (let/<u>make</u>) you do stupid, unnecessary things.

6 They (don't make/<u>don't let</u>) you have any free time to relax.

7 They (<u>make</u>/let) you obey stupid orders, just to teach you discipline.

8 The worst thing is, nobody (<u>lets</u>/makes) you think for yourself.

b) *What do your parents make you do or not make you do? What do they let you do or not let you do? Write a short text in your exercise book. You can use these ideas and add your own:*

homework • housework • pay your mobile bill[1] • work for extra money • write thankyou letters • clean your room • help in the kitchen • go to church • pay back money that you borrowed • sleep longer at the weekends • invite your friends whenever you want • stay out late • watch TV until late in the week

5013

14 What have they had done? (have something done) ▶ p. 92

a) *Before and after. What **have** they **had done**?*

hair – dye[2]

hair – cut

computer – repair

She's <u>*had her hair dyed.*</u>

He <u>*'s had his hair cut.*</u>

They <u>*'ve had the/their computer repaired.*</u>

b) *What do you and your family sometimes **have done** or **never have done** (**every day/week, once a month/year**)? Write sentences.*

1 hair/cut: *I have my hair cut about once every two months/once a year.*

2 car/wash: *My dad /mum never has our car washed. He/She washes it himself/herself.*

3 pizza/deliver: *When I'm at my friend's house, we sometimes have a pizza delivered.*

4 eyes/test: *I wear glasses, so I have my eyes tested twice a year. / I've never had my eyes tested.*

5014 5 computer/repair: *I've only had my computer repaired once. / I've never had my computer repaired.*

[1] bill [bɪl] *Rechnung*   [2] dye [daɪ] *färben*

15 MEDIATION International work camps ▶ *p. 93* • *WB (p. 79)*

Tell a British exchange student the main facts from the following website information: who takes part in the work camp programmes, how long you stay, what kind of work you do, how long you work, free-time activities, etc. Make notes in English in your exercise book first.

Internationale *work camps* für Teenager

Wer, wo und wann?
Jedes Jahr nehmen junge Leute aus aller Welt an Hilfsprojekten in internationalen *work camps* in über hundert Ländern teil. Dabei lernen die Teilnehmer/innen nicht nur andere Länder und Kulturen kennen. Bei einem Aufenthalt von 2 bis 6 Wochen arbeiten sie zusammen an einem sinnvollen Projekt. Die Camps finden meist in den Monaten Juni bis September für die Altersgruppen von 14 bis 19 Jahren statt.

Arbeitsgruppen und Arbeitsbereiche
In jeder *Work-camp*-Gruppe sind 10 bis höchstens 20 Teilnehmer/innen, die jeden Tag ca. vier Stunden mit einem/einer Gruppenleiter/in zusammen arbeiten. Die Arbeitsbereiche sind vielfältig, z.B. Umweltprojekte, die Betreuung von Kindern, Englischunterricht, Mitarbeit in Krankenhäusern oder Waisenhäusern, die Renovierung von Schulen, Jugendzentren und Spielplätzen oder historischen Gebäuden. Die Campsprache ist meist Englisch.

Unterbringung und Freizeit
Unterkünfte, z.B. in Jugendzentren oder Jugendherbergen werden gestellt. Auch die Verpflegung ist kostenfrei. Oft wird nicht nur zusammen gegessen sondern unter Anleitung auch zusammen gekocht. Freizeitaktivitäten kommen auch nicht zu kurz. Zum Freizeitprogramm gehören nicht nur gemeinsame Ausflüge und Sightseeing, sondern auch Workshops. Viel Sport sowie Fahrradtouren und Wanderungen gehören auch dazu.

WB, pp. 70–71

---

16 READING WORKING WITH THE TEXT The caller ▶ *pp. 94–97* • *WB (pp. 77–78)*

a) *How well do you know the story? Read the summary carefully. Some details are not correct. Mark wrong sentences, sentence parts or words.*

Lindsay's Aunt Margaret has died. After the funeral Lindsay's dad can't find his cellphone. Later at home, when Lindsay gets a call from a voice that says it's Aunt Margaret, she thinks it's her friend Candice who is playing a trick on her. Lindsay goes to Missy's party and wears Aunt Margaret's diamond earrings to make the other girls jealous. When the voice of Aunt Margaret calls Lindsay again on her father's cellphone, Lindsay thinks it's her brothers who are playing a trick. Lindsay tells the voice that she was only nice to her because she wanted her earrings. That evening all the girls stay at Missy's house. Lindsay gets a third call from the unknown caller on her father's cellphone. The voice says she's coming back to get the earrings. Lindsay thinks it's her brothers again who have found the phone and are trying to scare her. Lindsay calls home, but her mom says the boys are playing cards. In the middle of the call the lights go out at Lindsay's house and there's a loud noise. Then someone knocks at the back door of Missy's house. Lindsay is scared. She wants Missy to look who is at the door. Missy leaves Lindsay alone upstairs. Then Lindsay's phone rings again. She hears a knock on the window and is afraid that it's Aunt Margaret's ghost. The voice behind the bedroom door sounds like Missy's, laughing at Lindsay because she's crying like a baby. Angry with Missy, Lindsay opens the door, but it is not Missy who is holding the phone in a muddy hand…

---

b) *Some things happen in the story that can't be explained in a logical way. Find examples of this in the text and write what happens in your own words. Give the line numbers and write in your exercise book.*

WB, pp. 58–62

c) *Do you think this is a good story? What makes it good? Or: Why don't you find the story good? Explain. Write in your exercise book.*

17 My book quiz ▶ *p. 97*

a) How well do you know your student's book? Test yourself! Write short answers.

1. The capital of Australia is …   *Canberra*

2. Who claimed Australia for Britain in 1788?   *Captain James Cook*

3. The name of the famous rock that is important to Aboriginal culture is …   *Uluru /Ayers Rock*

4. In which year did Australia become independent?   *1901*

5. What's another word for the Australian dry land?   *the outback*

6. The kind of football that Australians play is called …   *Aussie rules*

7. The paper that tells employers about your education and work experience is called your …   *CV*

8. In the USA your 'CV' is called a '…'   *résumé*

9. What is the UK equivalent[1] of German 'Abitur'?   *A-levels*

10. When was the Constitution of the United States signed?   *1789*

11. When was the U.N. Universal Declaration of Human Rights passed?   *1948*

12. The first ten amendments to the US Constitution are known as …   *the Bill of Rights*

13. How old must you be to run for the office of US President?   *35*

14. What does 'ASBO' mean?   *anti-social behaviour order*

15. ASBOs are given by …   *UK courts*

16. In the USA young troublemakers can choose to go to … instead of prison.   *boot camp*

17. What is the English word for 'gemeinnützige Arbeit'?   *community service*

b) Think carefully about what you have learned in your student's book. Then match the pictures below to the units 1–4. Write the unit number under the picture.

3

4

1

2

[1] equivalent [ɪˈkwɪvələnt] *Entsprechung*

How well can you do these things?

	Very well	OK	Practise!

LISTENING AND READING SKILLS: I can…

… understand the song text *Get up, stand up*. _____ ☐ ☐ ☐

… understand a news report in American English. _____ ☐ ☐ ☐

… read a book review which gives a summary and opinion, e.g. the review of the novel *Speak* (SB p. 54). _____ ☐ ☐ ☐

… read a poem loudly and clearly to an audience, e.g. *The British* (SB p. 66). ___ ☐ ☐ ☐

… read longer fictional and non-fictional texts without difficulty, e.g. *The caller* (SB pp. 94–96), *Eighteen-year-old mayor* (SB p. 60). _____ ☐ ☐ ☐

SPEAKING AND WRITING SKILLS: I can…

… give an oral summary of a film or TV programme using only information about the events, not personal opinion. _____ ☐ ☐ ☐

… talk about politics and human rights using suitable vocabulary. _____ ☐ ☐ ☐

… summarize the main points of a non-fictional text. _____ ☐ ☐ ☐

… write an argumentative text, giving arguments and examples for and against a statement, then summing up the main points with my personal opinion, e.g. on the use of mobiles at school. _____ ☐ ☐ ☐

MEDIATION SKILLS: I can…

… summarize and report a conversation or written text from German into English or from English into German in my own words, e.g. information about international work camps. _____ ☐ ☐ ☐

TOPICS: I have learned…

… about the Universal Declaration of Human Rights. _____ ☐ ☐ ☐

… about teenage activities, interests and hobbies, e.g. mobile behaviour, relationships, volunteer work and community service. _____ ☐ ☐ ☐

… about problems of teenagers who behave anti-socially and about punishments for anti-social behaviour, e.g. ASBOs and boot camps. _____ ☐ ☐ ☐

STUDY AND LANGUAGE SKILLS: I know…

… how to use an online dictionary. _____ ☐ ☐ ☐

… how an author can create suspense in a literary text. _____ ☐ ☐ ☐

HOW I COULD IMPROVE MY ENGLISH SKILLS: I could…

(e.g. work through parts of Skills Check 2 again, read the Skills File in my SB in detail…)

_____

_____

_____

_____

_____

Skills Training

LISTENING

In this part of your workbook you will find exercises that will help you with your skills: listening, reading, writing, speaking, mediation.

1 School chat (Listening for gist) ▶ WB (p. 77) 🎧16

Listen to four short dialogues. What are the friends talking about?
Match the letters A–D to the correct topic.

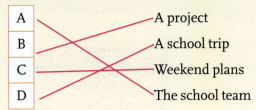

A	A project
B	A school trip
C	Weekend plans
D	The school team

Tip 1

Think about the four topics. Which **words/word fields** might you expect to hear? Listen for those words.
For example:
project > research, subject, finish
school trip > bus/train, place, time
weekend plans > friends, party
school team > match, game, play

2 The Olympic Games (Listening for gist) ▶ WB (p. 77) 🎧17

Read statements A–E. Then listen to four students talking about the Olympic Games. Match the correct statement to each student. There is one statement that you do not need.

A I'm a sporty person, so I love the summer Olympics.

B I think the Olympic Games have become too political.

C The Games have become too spectacular and too expensive.

D I'm not into sport, so I don't really follow the Games on TV.

E It's great that Olympic athletes are so disciplined and work so hard.
   We can all learn from such people.

Tip 2

Before you listen, concentrate[1] on the statements.
Decide which are **positive** and which are **negative**.
When you listen, notice how the speakers give their opinion. Is their tone of voice positive or negative?

5402 Student 1: *E*   Student 2: *A*   Student 3: *D*   Student 4: *C*

3 Tricky numbers, times, letters (Listening for detail) ▶ WB (p. 77) 🎧18

Listen and mark what you hear: one of each pair.

a) Numbers:

| 245 / 254 | 14 / 40 | 98 / 89 | 60 / 16 |

| 02256691 / 02256651 | 1978 / 1987 |

Tip 3

When you listen the first time, write down **names**, **places**, **dates**, **numbers**, **times** or **letters** exactly. They are easily confused.
For example: 30 or 13? 7E or 7A?
When you listen a second time, check your notes and concentrate on the answers you still need.

b) Times: | 2.30 / 2.13 | 12.30 / 1.30 | 4.30 / 3.30 | 9.15 / 9.50 |

5403 *c)* Letters: | A / E | E / I | A / R | G / J | J / G |

4 At the station (Listening for detail) ▶ WB (p. 77) 🎧19

You are going to hear three short train announcements. First read the statements below carefully. Then listen to the announcements and decide whether the statements are true or false. Tick a box.

	True	False
1 The train to Edinburgh will leave from platform 6.	✔	
2 Departure will be delayed by 13 minutes.		✔
3 The 12.15 train to Bristol will not leave from platform 9 today.	✔	
4 The Bristol train will now leave from platform 7E.		✔
5 The train from York will now arrive at platform 3 at 12.43.		✔

5404

[1] concentrate [ˈkɒnsntreɪt] *sich konzentrieren*

5 The London Eye (Listening for detail) ▶ WB (p. 77) 🎧 20

Listen to a guide telling tourists about the London Eye. Then choose the correct answer, A, B or C.

1 The tourists' ride on the Eye is booked[1] for …

| A | 2.30 pm. | B✓ | 3.30 pm. | C | 4.30 pm. |

2 How far can you see on a clear day?

| A | 40 miles. | B✓ | 40 kilometres. | C | 14 kilometres. |

3 When did work on the London Eye start?

| A | 1990. | B | 1991. | C✓ | 1992. |

4 How many passenger capsules[2] are there?

| A | 23. | B | 25. | C✓ | 32. |

5 The London Eye is now the … biggest wheel in the world.

| A | second | B | third | C✓ | fourth |

5505

Tip 4

Often information is given **indirectly**, in different words. For example:
'When did work on the Eye start?'
You hear only:
'It took *7* years to build and it was opened in *1999*.' But you can work out the answer from this information.

6 BE and AE (BE and AE pronunciation) ▶ WB (p. 77) 🎧 21–23

a) *Listen to the words (🎧 22). Is the pronunciation BE or AE? Write A (American) or B (British).*

1	*B*	5	*A*	9	*B*
2	*A*	6	*A*	10	*A*
3	*B*	7	*B*	11	*A*
4	*A*	8	*A*	12	*B*

5506

Tip 5

	BE	AE
grass, can't	[ɑ:]	[æ]
knew, Tuesday	[ju:]	[u:]
not, got	[ɒ]	[ɑ]
first, world, more	➤ in AE you hear the 'r'	
little, city, writer	➤ in AE 't' in the middle of a word sounds like 'd'	

b) *Now look carefully at the sentences below. Mark the sounds which are pronounced differently in AE. Then listen (🎧 23) and check that you have marked all the differences. You'll hear each sentence twice: first in BE then in AE.*

1 It's so hot in here! Let's go to the park! I'll ask my sister if she wants to join us.

2 Let's have a nice cool drink first. How about a glass of mineral water? Or some coffee?

3 I forgot to tell you. We have a new student in our class. It's her birthday soon. She's invited us all to a party.

c) *You are in a tourist information office in London. Listen (🎧 24) to what people are asking. Are they British or American? Write the numbers of the speakers under the right flag.*

Speakers   *2, 5, 7*   Speakers   *1, 3, 4, 6, 8*

[1] book [bʊk] *buchen, reservieren*   [2] capsule ['kæpsju:l] *Kapsel*

7 At the youth hostel (Accents) ▶ WB (p. 77) 🎧 24

You hear some young people talking about why tourists like to visit their countries. Do they come from the UK, the USA or Australia? Write the country under the photo.

5607

1 UK   2 Australia   3 USA   4 Australia   5 USA   6 UK

8 Problems (Fast speech) ▶ WB (p. 77) 🎧 25, 26

a) *Listen (🎧 25) to three teenagers talking about their problems. They talk at a normal speed, but in everyday speech some words are shortened or missed out. Listen for the forms in* **Tip 6** *too. Who says what? Write the names in 1–4 below: Todd, Will or Liz.*

1   Todd   and   Liz   are having problems with parents.

2   Todd   's parents are not so strict with his younger brother.

3   Will   doesn't know how to solve his problem with his girlfriend.

4   Liz   is having problems at school with her grades.

> **Tip 6**
>
> When people talk quickly, they may use expressions that are not grammatically correct. You hear the following forms especially in AE. Maybe you've heard these forms in song lyrics too:
>
> | | | |
> |---|---|---|
> | **gonna** | > | 'going to' |
> | **wanna** | > | 'want to' |
> | **gotta** | > | 'have got to' |
> | **kinda** | > | 'kind of' |
> | **dunno** | > | 'don't know' |

b) *Listen (🎧 26) to the rest of the conversation. This time the friends talk faster. Listen carefully for short or ungrammatical forms. Then tick true or false.*

	True	False
1 Liz doesn't want to give up her weekend job.	✔	
2 Liz thinks she'll talk to her Math teacher and her Science teacher.		✔
3 Will's girlfriend is called Katie.		✔
4 Will doesn't always work on Friday evenings.	✔	
5 Will has a job at a pizza place.		✔
6 Will has a friend called Matt.	✔	
7 Will's girlfriend went to a movie with a boy called Stevie.		✔
8 Todd says Will has to trust[1] his girlfriend more.	✔	

[1] trust [trʌst] *(ver)trauen*

9 Talking about jobs (Listening skills) ▶ WB (p. 77) 🎧 27

a) *Listen to five young people talking about jobs. First, read the statements below and the list of names. Then listen to what they say. Choose the correct statement below for each person. Write A–E next to the names.*

A 'I've found a job as a waitress[1] in a café, but I won't find out details until I call again later today.'

B 'I had a big problem on my first day. The manager wasn't very happy.'

C 'I've applied for some jobs I got from the job centre. I've had just one job offer so far.'

D 'I enjoy my work now, but at first I wasn't allowed to serve[2] customers[3] because I had to learn the job.'

E 'I wanted to work with computers, but I'm learning to repair cars now. I like it.'

1 Dylan: [C]   2 Sophie: [A]   3 Gina: [D]

4 Jamie: [E]   5 Leo: [B]

b) *Now listen again, this time for detail. Choose the correct answer and tick the box.*

1 Dylan is looking for …

☐ a summer job.   ☐ a job after school.   ✔ a Saturday job.

2 Dylan found some jobs at the job centre, and he has applied for …

☐ four.   ✔ five.   ☐ six.

3 Sophie already has some job experience …

☐ in a hotel.   ☐ in a café.   ✔ in a restaurant.

4 Sophie has to call again about the job at …

☐ 1.30.   ✔ 2.30.   ☐ 3.30.

5 Gina is from …

✔ Australia.   ☐ the UK.   ☐ the USA.

6 Gina works in a flower shop …

☐ from nine to five.   ✔ from nine to six.   ☐ after school.

7 Jamie has a …

☐ part-time job.   ☐ holiday job.   ✔ full-time job.

8 Jamie works in …

☐ Glasgow.   ✔ Aberdeeen.   ☐ a village near Aberdeen.

9 Leo has been working in a travel agency …

✔ for a week.   ☐ for a month.   ☐ since he left school.

10 Leo sent the wrong flight tickets to Mrs White. She wanted to go to …

☐ Johannesburg.   ✔ Hawaii.   ☐ Alaska.

---

[1] waitress ['weɪtrəs] *Kellnerin*   [2] serve [sɜːv] *bedienen*   [3] customer ['kʌstəmə] *Kunde/-in*

READING

10 ESL in L.A. (1) (Skimming) ▶ WB (p. 78)

You would like to visit Los Angeles and maybe do an English course. You find this information on the internet. Would it be useful to you? Who is the information for? **Skim** *the text for a few seconds. Then tick A, B or C.*

The information is for …

| A | teachers of ESL. |

| B | American college students. |

| C̶ | foreign[1] students of English. |

ESL in L.A.	
ESL programs	Our programs cover all areas of English as a second language. We offer intensive programs and exam preparation programs for college and university entrance.
Course levels	We offer courses for **beginners**, **intermediate** and **advanced** levels[2]. All levels offer training in reading, listening, speaking and writing skills, vocabulary building, pronunciation and grammar. Courses in **American culture**, English for **business and commerce**, English for **science and technology** are offered at intermediate and advanced levels only.
Course hours	9 am–12 am, 2 pm–5 pm or 6 pm–9 pm, Mon–Fri. There are no weekend courses.
Course groups	**Intensive programs**: groups of 6–8 students. All other course groups: 12–15 students.
Teaching staff	All our teachers are college and university trained professionals and are **native speakers**.
Location	Centrally located close to city attractions, shopping and eating within walking distance.
Accommodation	Students may choose to stay with a selected **host family** or at a **residence club** (single room, with breakfast and dinner).

5810

Tip 7

Step 1: Look at the **form** of the text. Is it a newspaper article, a fictional text, an information brochure?

Step 2: Look at the **title**, **headings** and **pictures**.

Step 3: Look at the words in **bold** type.

11 ESL in L.A. (2) (Scanning) ▶ WB (p. 78)

Now scan the text in exercise 10 to find the answers to these questions. The key words are in **bold** *for you. Write notes.*

1 What does '**ESL**' mean?   *English as a second language*

2 How many **course levels** are offered?   *3*

3 Do all courses teach **American culture**?   *no*

4 **Where** is the school?   *central, close to attractions/shops*

5 Are there any courses at the **weekend**?   *no*

6 How many students are there in the **intensive** program groups?   *6–8*

7 How many kinds of **accommodation** does the school help with?   *2*

8 Which meals are given with the **accommodation**?   *breakfast and dinner*

5811

Tip 8

Concentrate only on the **key words** in the questions when you scan. Read **around** a key word to find the answers. Remember, you may find a key word in different places in the text, not just in one.

[1] foreign ['fɒrɪn] *ausländisch*   [2] advanced level [əd'vɑːnsd] *fortgeschrittenes Niveau*

12 Getting into London (Marking key words; taking notes) ▶ WB (p. 78)

a) You need information about different kinds of transport into London from Heathrow Airport. Choose and mark key words for the most important information.

Getting into London from Heathrow

From Heathrow Airport you can take a train, the tube, a coach or a taxi into London.

1 If you want to go by train, the Heathrow Express takes you to Paddington Station in just 15–20 minutes. Trains run every 15 minutes. Cost: £16.50.

2 By tube the journey takes 45 minutes. Heathrow is on the Piccadilly line. There are three tube stations at the airport serving[1] different terminals. The tube stops at famous places in the capital such as Hyde Park Corner, Piccadilly Circus and Covent Garden. Tube trains leave every five minutes. Cost: £4.50.

3 You can take the National Express coach from the Central Bus Station (near Terminals 1, 2 and 3) to Victoria Coach Station in central London. The journey by coach takes 45–75 minutes. There are three to six buses an hour. Cost: £5.

4 By taxi the journey takes 30–75 minutes. Cost for up to five passengers: £40–70.

(Prices: February 2010)

b) A friend asks you what you have found out. Use your key words to make short notes to tell your friend.

1 train: Heathrow Express>Paddington, 15–20 min., every 15 min., £16.50

2 tube: Piccadilly line, three tube stations at airport, 45 min., £4.50

3 coach: National Express, Central Bus Station to Victoria Coach Station, 45–75 min., £5

4 taxi: 30–75 min., £40–70

13 Florida's Marine Park (Reading for detail) ▶ WB (p. 78)

Before you read the text about Marine Park, read the statements on the next page. Mark key words in the statements. Look for the answers and tick true, false or not given.

Tip 9

If there are no or not many words in **bold** in the text, choose your own key words from the questions. Look for them when you scan the text and read **around** them.

Opening times
Marine Park is open to visitors every day from 9 am to 7 pm, and from 9 am to 9 pm in the summer months and at holiday times.

How to get here
If you are driving, you will find us just 10 miles northwest of downtown Tampa. From Tampa International Airport it's just a 20-minute taxi ride. Our main entrance and car park for 3,500 vehicles are on South Marine Drive. You can't miss us! Please visit our website for detailed directions.

Admission
1-Day tickets: adults $83.95 (plus tax[2]), children (3–10) years $69.95 (plus tax). Children two years and under go free. There are discounts for senior citizens. Please show your ID.
Online tickets: For tickets bought online 7 days in advance, there is a standard price of $69.95 (plus tax). You can print your ticket at home and there's no waiting at the park entrance.
Florida visitors: Please see our special online offers for 1-day and 3-day tickets.
Florida residents[3]: Please see our special annual and vacation offers.

5913

[1] serve [sɜːv] *bedienen*   [2] tax [tæks] *Steuer*   [3] resident [rezɪdənt] *Bewohner/in*

	True	False	Not given
1 The park is open all year round from 9 am to 9 pm.		✔	
2 Marine Park is 10 miles northwest of Tampa.	✔		
3 It's a 30-minute drive from Tampa International Airport.		✔	
4 You enter Marine Park from South Marine Drive.	✔		
5 Adult tickets are cheaper online.	✔		
6 There is no US tax on tickets.		✔	
7 You can use online tickets for one year.			✔
8 There are special ticket offers for Florida residents.	✔		
9 You can buy Quick Queue tickets.			✔
10 Children under three years of age are free.	✔		

14 Marine Park visitor information (Reading for detail) ▶ WB (p. 78)

Read the visitor information sign carefully. It is not important to understand all the words when you read the first time. Complete the sentences below with words from the text.

Marine Park Visitor Information

Please note that before you enter the park, all bags will be examined by our security staff. It is not permitted[1] to bring sharp[2] or dangerous objects into the park, including pocket knives, cans and glass bottles. Please leave these objects in your vehicle.

Visitors are asked not to bring food and drinks into the park. Restaurants and stands selling snacks and soft drinks can be found in several park areas. Exception: baby food and food for special diets.

Visitors are reminded that all indoor areas of the park are smoke-free. Outdoor smoking areas are clearly marked on your park map. If you wish to smoke, please do so in these areas only.

Information about animal feeding times can be found in the park map. Please do not try to feed the animals. It's bad for the animals and may be dangerous for you.

If you wish to bring along your pets, they can wait for you in our air-conditioned pets' area near the main entrance. Please walk your dog at regular intervals during your park visit and bring along enough pet food for the length of your stay. Our pet service costs just $12 a day.

Please note: For safety reasons, visitors are not allowed to bring objects into the park which are __sharp__ or __dangerous__ . You can buy soft drinks and snacks in the park, so you are asked not to bring your own __food and drinks__ . __Smoking__ is only permitted in some areas.

Please follow the signs. Details of __animal feeding times__ can be found in the __park map__ .

There's also a service that looks after visitors' __pets__ , so you can bring along your dog or cat too – for just $12 a day.

> **Tip 10**
>
> The words in the task are often different from the words in the text. But the meaning is the same.
> Try to work out the meaning of the unknown words from the context.

[1] permit [pə'mɪt] *gestatten* [2] sharp [ʃɑːp] *scharf*

15 What does it mean? (Working out the meaning of words) ▶ WB (p. 77)

Look at the text in exercise 14 again. How did you work out the meaning of words that are new? Write the words below in the lists with their German meaning. Some words fit in two lists. Decide what helped you most.

exception • examined • *staff* • length • vehicle • stand • diet • air-conditioned • entrance • intervals

... from the context	... like a German word	... from a part of the word or from the word family
staff — Personal	vehicle — Vehikel, Fahrzeug	exception — Ausnahme
length — Länge	stand — Stand	examined — kontrolliert,
air-conditioned – klimatisiert	diet — Diät	überprüft
	intervals – Intervalle, Abstände	entrance – Einfahrt, Eingang

6115

16 Saving our planet (Reading skills) ▶ WB (pp. 77–78)

This is part of a text about the earth's problems. Read it carefully. It is not important to understand all the words the first time you read.

Saving our planet

1 Climate change is thought by scientists to be a major problem. In less than a hundred years from now, the earth's average temperature could have risen by as much as five degrees. People living in cold countries may like the idea, but the temperature rise would put the earth and its peoples in danger, as a warmer climate would have disastrous effects on the future of man and nature.

2 A main cause is that humans produce 'greenhouse gases', for example, when burning oil, gas or wood for energy. Industries are a major cause of this. CO2 is released into the atmosphere. This leads to the 'greenhouse effect', as the sun's heat is trapped by too many greenhouse gases in the atmosphere, so the earth gets warmer. Deforestation is another cause, as forests and rainforests absorb carbon dioxide.

3 The effects of global warming could be catastrophic. The ice at the poles could melt, so sea levels would rise – maybe by up to two metres in the next 150 years, some experts believe. This would mean that cities like New York, London or Tokyo might slowly disappear under the sea. Millions of people could be permanently homeless. Some countries could become seriously overpopulated. There may be more natural disasters, like tsunamis and tornadoes. Tropical diseases would spread more quickly into non-tropical countries. The heat could dry up the food we grow. Food prices would rise and millions could become hungry. There might not be enough drinking water, so wars might start. Some animals and plants might die out because they could not survive in saltwater.

4 In order to slow down climate change, we must reduce global warming, for example, by using less energy in our daily lives. We should stop burning oil and gas, which produce carbon dioxide and are non-renewable. We should use more renewable energy like solar or wind power. We should save electricity and water, and produce less waste by recycling. We could buy recyclable and energy-efficient products (light bulbs, fridges, computers, etc.). We could plant more trees. We must stop cutting down rainforests. All this and much more ...

a) Choose a heading for each paragraph. Write A–D after the numbers.

1 **B**   2 **D**   A Solutions[1]   C Consequences

3 **C**   4 **A**   B Problems   D Reasons

b) Look at the text again. How can you work out the meaning of words that are new? Write the words in the box in the lists 1–3 below with their German meaning. Some words fit in two lists. Decide what helped you most.

> release • absorb • greenhouse gas • poles • melt • disaster • deforestation
> overpopulation • tropical • major • renewable • recyclable • energy-efficient • rainforest

1 I can understand these words from the **context**: *release (abgeben), greenhouse gas (Treibhausgas), melt (schmelzen), major (bedeutend, groß)*

2 These words are like **German** words: *absorb, poles, disaster, tropical, energy-efficient*

3 I know **part** of these words or a word from the **word family**: *renewable, recyclable, deforestation, overpopulation, rainforest*

c) Read the statements carefully. Is the information true, false or not in the text? Tick a box.

	True	False	Not in the text
1 At the end of this century the earth's temperature could be a few degrees warmer.	✔		
2 Households produce about a third of carbon dioxide.			✔
3 Carbon dioxide is a 'greenhouse gas'.	✔		
4 Natural gas is a renewable source of energy.		✔	
5 A lot of the waste that we produce every day finds its way into the seas and oceans.			✔
6 Recyclable products help to reduce waste.	✔		
7 Rainforests are burned down so that cattle farmers can produce more meat for export.			✔
8 CO2 cannot be absorbed.		✔	

d) Now complete these sentences with information from the text.

1 Climate change is thought to be a major problem because *a warmer climate could change the life of humans and nature./... a warmer climate could put the earth in danger.*

2 We all produce 'greenhouse gases' by *burning oil, gas or wood for energy.*

3 The earth is getting warmer because *the sun's heat is trapped by greenhouse gases in the atmosphere.*

4 If the ice at the poles melted, *sea levels would rise* . As a result *cities like New York, London or Tokyo might slowly disappear under the sea.*

5 Maybe people would not have enough to eat because the *heat could dry up the food we grow.*

6 Wars might break out because *there might not be enough drinking water.*

[1] solution [səˈluːʃn] *Lösung*

WRITING

17 Collecting ideas (Brainstorming) ▶ WB (pp. 80, 81–82)

a) *Choose three topics from A–F below. Brainstorm ideas that you could use in an e-mail to a friend. Make a list or a mind map for each of your three topics in your exercise book.*

A	My free-time activities	D	Work experience
B	My favourite magazine	E	My best birthday
C	My ideal job	F	Raising money for charities

Tip 11
Remember to cross out ideas you won't use and number the useful ideas.

My free-time activities
2 *sports*
 football training
 ~~*skateboarding*~~
 basketball team
1 *friends*
 shopping
 texting
 parties
 hanging out
3 *homework*

b) *Use your notes from a) to write an e-mail to an English-speaking friend about one of your topics. Write 80–100 words in your exercise book.*

Hi ...!
Thanks for your last mail. You wanted to know about what I do in my free time. Well, I expect I do the same as you – I often spend time with my friends. Sometimes we go to the local shopping mall and look at CDs and DVDs ...

18 Giving information (The 5 Ws) ▶ WB (pp. 81–82)

a) *A good text gives the reader important information about who, what, where, when and why. The text below reports a street accident. In what order does it answer the 5 Ws?*

Tip 12
The **5 Ws** are important, both in reading and writing.
In a good story/report, etc, you find answers to most of the **5 Ws** in the first two or three sentences. *Why... ?* and *How...?* sometimes come later.
The **order** of the information is not important and can be different from text to text.

Teenager hit by cyclist[1]

At 10.30 last night a 15-year-old girl was hurt by a cyclist as she was crossing Radfield Road on her way home after visiting a friend. The cyclist, who admitted[2] that he was riding fast on the empty road, ran into the girl, who was wearing dark clothes. The cyclist said, 'She came from nowhere. I just didn't see her.' The cyclist called an ambulance and the girl was treated for a broken finger and shock.

1 *When? – at 10.30 last night*

2 *Who? – a 15-year-old girl*

3 *What? – was hurt by a cyclist*

4 *Where? – Radfield Road*

6318
5 *Why? – the cyclist was riding too fast, he didn't see the girl*

b) *Now write a short text about your last school trip, or your last holiday. Give information about the 5 Ws in the first few sentences, as in the text in a). Write 80–100 words in your exercise book.*

Last year in ... our class went on a trip to .... with...../Our last class trip took place in ... this year ...

---

[1] cyclist ['saɪklɪst] *Radfahrer/in*   [2] admit [əd'mɪt] *zugeben*

19 Making changes ▸ WB (pp. 81–82)

a) *Here are some tips that will help you when you want to write a text.*
Read **Tip 13** *and study the following sentences carefully.*

Tip 13

You can:
- change active to passive or passive to active.
- add a subordinate clause.
- change direct to indirect speech.
- make one sentence out of two using a linking word.
- change the linking word, e.g. *so > because, but > although.*

1 After three days the police caught the escaped prisoner. They had been told where they could find him.
Change active to passive and passive to active.
The escaped prisoner was caught after a few days. Someone had told the police where to find him.

2 It was a cold day in winter when Leila packed her bags and left home to start a new life in Pakistan. She had never met the man she was going to marry.
Add a relative clause – *where…* , and make one sentence out of two.
On a cold winter day Leila left home for Pakistan, where she would start a new life with a husband she had never met.

3 'I'll never be able to wear jeans and tops again, no trainers either,' Leila thought sadly.
Change direct to indirect speech; use group words, not details – *western clothes for jeans, tops, trainers.*
Leila was sad that she would never be able to wear western clothes again.

4 After breakfast, Rob and Pete started their bike tour. The sun was shining. There was a warm breeze and only a few white clouds in the sky.
Make one sentence out of two with a linking word, here: *When…* ; leave out details of weather description.
When Rob and Pete started their cycle tour in the morning, the weather was very good.

5 Tom always needs money, so he does a newspaper round before school and he sometimes works in his cousin's café on Wilmore Street after school. He washes cars and does garden work for the neighbours.
Change the linking word – *so > because.* Leave out job details.
Because Tom always needs money, he does lots of jobs before and after school.

b) *Now rewrite the following sentences and shorten them where possible. Make one sentence. Remember to use what you have read in a) above.*

1 It was really cold in the house, so Polly made a big pot of hot tea for everybody.

Polly made some hot tea because it was cold in the house.

2 US border police send back hundreds of illegal Mexican immigrants every month. Pedro was one of them.

Pedro was one of the illegal Mexican immigrants who are sent back at the border every month.

3 Jerry arrived late at the airport because of the traffic on the motorway. He found that his plane to Vancouver had already left.

When Jerry finally arrived at the airport, his plane to Vancouver had left.

4 'There's so much to prepare before the visitors arrive – the flat to clean, shopping to do, food to cook,' thought Emily nervously.

Emily was nervous because there was so much to do before the visitors arrived.

5 The climbers knew that they would be in serious difficulties if the weather didn't improve.

The climbers knew they would have big problems unless the weather improved.

c) *Now summarize the following paragraphs taken from different text types. There are many possible ways to do this, but your text should have the main facts and be much shorter.*

1 From an article in a local newspaper:

> Local boy 19-year-old Josh Turner has come back from a trip of a lifetime. He spent September and October doing volunteer work on a sheep station in New South Wales, Australia. Josh said he wanted to do something really different – and he did. He enjoyed the new experience so much that he would like to go again next year …

Josh Turner has arrived home after spending two enjoyable months (doing volunteer work) on an Australian sheep station. He would like to go there again next year.

2 From an accident report:

> A 50-year-old man and his wife are in a critical condition[1] after their Toyota crashed into a Mercedes truck on the M4 motorway near Bracknell yesterday evening at about 10 o'clock. Roads were wet after heavy[2] rain and there were areas of thick fog. The injured couple were taken to hospital. The driver of the truck was unhurt. When questioned by the police, he said that he had suddenly seen the Toyota coming towards him on the wrong side of the road. He had tried to …

Last night a car and a truck crashed on the M4 near Bracknell. The two people in the car were badly hurt and are in hospital. The accident was probably caused by bad road conditions after heavy rain and fog.

3 From a novel:

> Sarah had never seen such an amazing sight before. Her heart beat loudly with excitement as she walked to the edge[3] of the canyon and looked down at the Colorado River more than one kilometre below. She couldn't believe how lucky she was to be able to visit this natural wonder …

Sarah was surprised at what she saw. She felt very excited when she looked over the edge of the canyon at the Colorado River a long way below. She thought that she was very lucky to be there.

20 An informal letter (Structuring a text)   ▶ WB (pp. 81–82)

Write to a friend about an interesting time that you remember well, for example a day trip, a birthday celebration, a camping trip, a visit to somewhere exciting, etc. Brainstorm your ideas first. Remember to start with the 5 Ws and to use paragraphs. Here are a few ideas. Write about 100 words in your exercise book.

Hi/Hello…!/Dear …
Thanks for your mail. You must have had a great time last weekend.
Did I tell you about …?
… is a fantastic place. There's so much … including … We had a lot of fun.
First we … after that we … , In the evening …
I have to stop now because …
Love, /Best wishes,

Tip 14

Give your text:
- a **beginning**. Say what you are going to write about. Start with an interesting opening sentence.
- a **middle**. Give details of events, etc. with a new paragraph for each new idea, starting with a general topic sentence.
- an interesting **end** and a personal closing sentence.

[1] condition [kən'dɪʃn] *Zustand*   [2] heavy [hevɪ] *stark, schwer*   [3] edge [edʒ] *Kante*

21 Writing a formal letter ▶ SF (p. 146)

a) Complete the text with words and phrases that are correct for formal letters.

You put your own address <u>*at the top on the right*</u>, but you don't write your name. Under your address

you write <u>*the date*</u>. The address of the person you are writing to is written <u>*on the left*</u>.

You begin a formal letter with '<u>*Dear Sir or Madam*</u>' when you don't know the name of the person

you are writing to. Remember that the first word of the first paragraph starts with a <u>*capital*</u>

letter – which is different from German. You shouldn't use <u>*short*</u> forms in formal letters. Write 'I
am' and 'I would' instead of 'I'm' and 'I'd'.

You finish a formal letter with '<u>*Yours faithfully*</u>' if you don't know the name of the person you

are writing to. If you know the name, you start with '<u>*Dear Mr/Mrs/Ms...*</u>' and you finish with

'<u>*Yours sincerely*</u>'.

*b) Lina Schneider from Munich writes a letter of application for a job as assistant receptionist[1] at a hotel in
London for six weeks in the summer. What belongs where in a formal letter? Choose the correct parts from the
list on the right and write the number in the correct place in the letter below.*

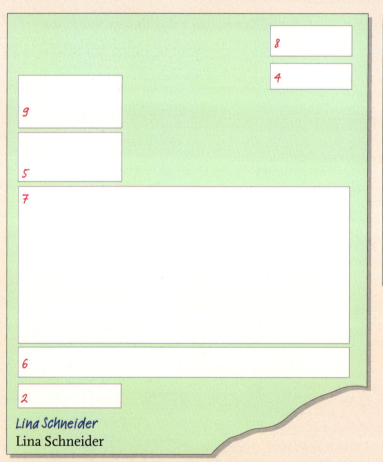

1 Best wishes
2 Yours faithfully
3 Dear Mrs Wilson
4 2nd May 2010
5 Dear Sir or Madam
6 I look forward to hearing from you.
7 I am writing to apply for the job of
   assistant receptionist as advertised
   on your website …
8 Webergasse 8
   81735 Munich
9 The Manager
   Lancaster Hall Hotel
   28 Lancaster Road
   London W8 IJL

Tip 15

Note that in British addresses the house
number comes **before** the name of the
road or street, not after it.
Note also that in the UK the postcode
comes **after** the town or city, not before it.

6621

*c) If you wanted this job, how would you write your letter of application? In your exercise book, write the main
text of your letter. Include the following:*

- your personal details
- how long you have been learning English and how good your English is
- what kind of person you are, work experience, your hobbies and interests
- why you would like the job and why you think you could do it well.

[1] receptionist [rɪˈsepʃənɪst] *Empfangsmitarbeiter/in*

22 Writing a CV ▶ *SF (p. 148)*

Lina has to enclose her CV with the application. Here is the necessary information about her:

> Her telephone number is 0049 89 612 37 97. Her mobile number is 0173 835 2380.
> Her e-mail is: lschneider@afl.com
> She was born in Munich on 23rd November 1995.
>
> Lina is a friendly, hard-working student who likes speaking English and enjoys meeting people. She is good at organizing and likes working in a team. She is punctual and reliable.
> She has already worked as a waitress[1] for six weeks in a hotel in Stockholm, Sweden, where she spoke English and German to hotel guests. Last year in the Easter holidays she also worked at the information desk in a shopping mall in Munich for two weeks.
> In her free time she likes reading and writing to online friends in the UK and the USA. She enjoys cooking, swimming and playing tennis. She is a member of the school drama club.
> Lina was at primary school in Augsburg from 2001 to 2005. She has been at secondary school in Munich since 2005. She is taking her school-leaving exams (similar to A-Levels) this year. She has a good level of everyday English (six years) and French (four years). She also has good computer skills and a moped licence.

a) *In what order should Lina present this information at the top of her CV? Write numbers 1–4 behind the headings.*

Postal address	2	E-mail address	4	Place of birth	6
Name	1	Mobile number	3	Date of birth	5

> **Tip 16**
> Date and place of birth are not always given in English CVs, but it is useful for employers to know your **age** and your **native language** if you are applying for a job abroad.
> The **personal statement** should not be longer than three short sentences. Use only long verb forms.

b) *What could Lina write in her short personal statement?*

I am a friendly, hard-working, punctual person who enjoys meeting people and speaking English. I am also a good organizer and a reliable team worker.

c) *In which order should she give details about the following? Write 1–6.*

Work experience	4	Hobbies and interests	5	Education	1
Qualifications	2	Reference(s)	6	Other skills	3

d) *Now use information in a) to write the CV sections in c), but leave out 'Reference(s)'. Remember to write notes, not full sentences.*

Education: *2001 – 2005 primary school in Augsburg, since 2005 secondary school in Munich*

Qualifications: *secondary school-leaving exams (similar to GCSEs) this year*

     Languages: English (six years), French (four years)

Other skills: *good computer skills, moped licence*

Work experience: *hotel waitress in Stockholm (6 weeks),*

     worked at information desk in a Munich shopping mall (2 weeks)

Hobbies and interests: *reading, writing to online friends in the UK and USA, cooking, swimming, playing tennis*

e) *Write the CV on the computer using the correct format.*

6722

---

[1] waitress ['weɪtrɪs] *Kellnerin*

SPEAKING

23 Asking for information (Question forms) ▶ WB (p. 79) 🎧 28

When you ask for information, it is important to form questions correctly and quickly. How do the teenagers ask the questions below? Write in your exercise book. Then listen to your CD (🎧 28) to check your answers.

Excuse me, *do you know where the buses leave from*, please?

a) *Dana is at JFK airport in New York. She wants a bus to the town centre.*

She asks someone politely …
- *if they know where the buses leave from*.
- where the buses stop in the town centre.
- how long the bus ride takes.
- how much bus tickets cost.
- where you buy the bus tickets.

What would I have to do exactly?

b) *Patrick is having an interview for a holiday job at a local IT company.*

He asks the interviewer …
- *what he would have to do exactly*.
- what time he would have to start.
- if he would have to work on Saturdays.
- how many hours he would have to work a week.
- when he could start.

6823

24 Describing a picture (Brainstorming vocabulary) ▶ WB (p. 79) • SF (p. 126) 🎧 29

When you describe a picture you usually have to …

- say generally where it is, e.g. *a scene in winter, a city street*.
- say where things/people are: *in the background/foreground/ middle, on the right/left, behind, in front of, between*.
- talk about the people (how many, what they are doing/wearing).
- say how the people are probably feeling or what they are thinking.
- use adjectives to talk about the atmosphere of the picture.

a) *Look at the picture below and in your exercise book, write down words to describe the scene. If you don't know the words you need, use your dictionary. Then describe the picture. You can record your speech.*

> **Tip 17**
>
> **Useful phrases for talking about pictures:**
> - *The picture shows a scene in summer/at a beach/in a big city/in the mountains …*
> - *It looks as if people are having fun …*
> - *The girl/boy on the right is laughing/ chatting …*
> - *Maybe she/he is thinking that …*
> - *She might be …*
> - *The people look/seem to be happy/ excited …*

> **Tip 18**
>
> **Answering questions**
> Give your opinion and find reasons and arguments for it.
> Here are some ideas:
> - *I can't ski so I think summer holidays are better.*
> - *In my opinion skiing holidays are too expensive …*
> - *… I prefer holidays where I can …*
> - *I like swimming and I'd like to learn to snowboard too because …*
> - *Sport plays an important role in my free time. I … every week …*

b) *Be prepared to answer general questions that have to do with the picture indirectly. Listen to the questions on your CD (🎧 29). Answer each question with at least three complete sentences. You can make notes in your exercise book first. Then practise your answers, first from your notes, then without your notes. Concentrate on speaking clearly, not too quickly.*

25 Comparing pictures   ▶ WB (p. 79) • SF (p. 126) 🎧 30

When you compare two pictures, talk about differences and compare advantages and disadvantages.

a) *Think of words and phrases to talk about the pictures below. Make lists:*

In a town	In the country
lots of people, cars, shops, noise,	few people, animals, forests, fields,
big buildings, dirty streets, dirty air,	paths, walking, hiking, hill-climbing,
loud, crowded, exciting, interesting,	little traffic, clean air, calm, quiet,
maybe nervous, unfriendly people,	healthy life, farms, no entertainment,
problems, traffic, accidents, police,	boring, not many jobs, no schools,
ambulance, offices, good public transport,	have to travel, no public transport
lots of entertainment	

b) *Use your notes in a) to discuss the two pictures. You can record your speech.*

c) *You often have to discuss two pictures or a given topic with your exam partner. Your dialogue should be realistic, so ask relevant questions. Here are some questions that you could ask about the topic of this exercise. Ask these questions in English, then check them on your CD (🎧 30):*

1 Wohnst du in der Stadt oder auf dem Land?

2 Wie lange wohnst du schon dort?

3 Würdest du lieber irgendwo anders wohnen?

4 Wie kommst du in die Schule?

5 Wo wohnen deine Freunde?

6 Welche Vorteile hat man auf dem Land?

7 Welche Vorteile hat man in der Stadt?

8 Hast du irgendwelche Großstädte im Ausland besucht?

9 Welche Großstadt hat dir am besten gefallen?

10 Wenn du nicht in Deutschland wohntest, wo würdest du wohnen wollen?

d) **Extra** *Ask your partner the questions 3–10 in c) in English.*

Tip 19

General tips:
- Don't answer questions with just *Yes* or *No* only. Better:
  Yes, I think so. No, I don't think so./ Yes, I do./Yes, it is. /No, it isn't, etc.
- If you repeat an idea or opinion, say it differently.
- What you say should be good English without too many mistakes.

Tip 20

If you don't understand what the examiner/interviewer says, it's good to know some useful, polite **phrases** by heart.
- *Could you repeat that, please?*
- *Could you explain that again/once more, please?*
- *Sorry, I can't quite follow you.*
- *Do you mean that I have to …?*
- *Sorry, what exactly do I have to do?*
- *Sorry, but I didn't quite understand/ catch what you said.*

Tip 21

Useful partner questions
When you have to talk to your exam partner, exchange information, give opinions, express feelings. You could start like this:
- *In my opinion, …*
- *I have read that …*
- *What do you think about …?*
- *Don't you think that …?*
- *Do you agree that …?*
- *Isn't it better to … than to …?*
- *What's your opinion about …?*

MEDIATION

26 London travel (Mediating a written text) ▶ WB (p. 79)

a) *You are going to visit London with your family and you want to tell them the best way to travel around the city. You find this information. Mark the main facts first. Then make notes below in German.*

Tip 22

Mark or underline the **main facts** and summarize them. Leave out details that are not important. Don't translate.

London Travelcards for international visitors

If you are planning to travel in and around London, it's best to buy a Travelcard. You will save money and you will have complete freedom[1] of travel on the Tube, buses, trams, Docklands Light Railway (DLR) and most local trains across the whole of London. You can even get riverboat tickets one third cheaper.

There are many different kinds of Travelcards. You have to choose whatever is best for you. You can buy a Travelcard for just one day, three days, seven days or even longer. London is divided into 6 travel zones and Travelcards cover different zones. Zones 1 and 2 cover Central London and most of the famous London sights. Zone 6 takes you to outer areas of the city. You must decide which zones you want to visit. Heathrow airport is in zone 6.

You must also know at what time you want to start your journey. If you plan to travel before 9.30 am (Mon–Fri), you will need a Peak Travelcard. If you travel after 9.30 am, you can buy an Off-Peak Travelcard, which is a little cheaper. For example, an Off-Peak One-day Travelcard for Zones 1 and 2 costs £5.60 for an adult (16 and over). By comparison, the Peak One-day Travelcard costs £7.20. Special reduced prices for children 5–15. Children under 5 go free. You can buy your Travelcard online, or all over the city at Tube stations, travel information centres and at some newsagents.
(Prices: February 2010)

Vorteile: Travelcard gültig für alle öffentlichen Verkehrsmittel in u. um

London, 30% Ermäßigung auf Bootsfahrkarten; Zonen: London hat 6

Fahrzonen: Zonen 1 u. 2 – Zentrum; Uhrzeit: wochentags billiger, nach

9.30 am: Off-Peak, vor 9.30 am: Peak; erhältlich für 1 Tag, 3 Tage, 7

Tage oder länger; Preisbeispiel: Erwachsene – 1 Tag Off-Peak, Zonen 1 u. 2 £5.60, (Peak £7.20)

Tip 23

When you mediate written information, the order is not important. Before you start, find the main points. Sometimes it's easier to mark key words and note information under headings, here: **advantages, travel zones, journey times, prices.**

b) *You tell your parents what you have found out, but they still have a few questions. Give short answers in German.*

1 Wo kann man die *Travelcard* kaufen? *online, in U-Bahn-Stationen, in Reisezentren, Kioske*

2 Kann man mit der *Travelcard* vom Flughafen in die Stadt fahren? *ja*

3 Du bist erst 16 und Schüler/in. Musst du schon den vollen Preis bezahlen? *ja*

4 Müssen wir für deinen Bruder zahlen? Er ist ja erst vier. *nein*

5 Wozu braucht man Zone 6? *für die äußeren Bezirke u. Heathrow Airport*

[1] freedom ['fri:dəm] *Freiheit*

27 What did he say? (Mediating what you hear) ▶ WB (p. 79) 🎧 31

You are at home, listening to a music programme on the radio. Explain what you hear (🎧 31) to your American exchange student. Use your own words and tell your friend the main things in a few sentences. You can make notes while you are listening, especially dates, places, etc.

> **Tip 24**
>
> Listen for details: **dates**, **place names** (cities and countries). Don't mediate opinions of the presenter. Make notes to help you remember.

Yes, he's talking about the 'Night Flyers'. They are coming to Germany on a concert tour at the end of March. Their first concert will be in Hamburg on 23rd March. The other concerts are in Berlin, Dresden and Stuttgart. The last concert is in Munich. You can buy tickets from tomorrow. After Germany they're going to Austria, Switzerland and Italy, and then to London for their last concert.

28 Explaining signs (Using modal auxiliaries) ▶ WB (p. 83)

You are in town with your dog, your bike and your British cousin. You want to explain these German signs to her. Complete with a modal (e. g. can, can't, must, mustn't, have to, etc.). More than one modal is sometimes possible.

> **Tip 25**
>
> **Don't confuse …!**
> you can't …
> *du kannst/darfst nicht …*
> you have to/you must …
> *du musst …*
> you don't have to …/you needn't …
> *du musst/brauchst nicht …*
> you mustn't …
> *du darfst nicht …*

1 🚫🐕 **WIR MÜSSEN DRAUßEN BLEIBEN**

We _can't/mustn't/aren't allowed to_ take the dog in there.

2 **PARKEN VERBOTEN** Fahrräder bitte nicht abstellen!

You _can't/mustn't/aren' t allowed to_ park your bike here.

3 Ganztägig geöffnet Tischreservierung nicht erforderlich

You _needn't/don't have to_ book a table.

4 Konzertkarten Bitte anstellen[1]

You _have to_ queue.

5 Betreten des Turms AUF EIGENE GEFAHR

You _can/may/are allowed to_ go up the tower, but at your own risk.

6 RUHEZONE! MOBILTELEFONE BITTE AUSSCHALTEN!

You _have to/must_ turn off your mobile.

7 STADTBIBLIOTHEK Haupteingang[2] wegen Renovierungsarbeiten geschlossen. Bitte Nebeneingang links um die Ecke benutzen.

We _can't/are not allowed to_ use the main entrance.

We _have to_ use the side entrance.

---

[1] queue [kjuː]   [2] main entrance [ˈmeɪn ˈentrəns]

LANGUAGE

29 A good story (Simple present or present progressive) ▶ GF (p. 154)

Trish is telling a friend about the film 'Australia'. Put the verbs in the simple present or present progressive.

'Well, the action takes place in northern Australia in 1939.

The war _is just starting_ (just, start). Kidman _plays_ (play)

Lady Sarah Ashley, an English aristocrat whose husband _owns_

(own) a huge farm and cattle station. Well, Sarah _flies_ (fly)

to Darwin to see what her husband _is doing_ (do) – she

believes (believe) he _is having_ (have) an affair.

When she _arrives_ (arrive), her husband's drover[1] _meets_ (meet) her to take her to the

farm – that's Jackman. On arrival they _find_ (find) her husband has been murdered, so now all

the land _belongs_ (belong) to her. Someone _tells_ (tell) her that the farm administrator[2]

is stealing (steal) her cattle and _is planning_ (plan) to take over her land, so – oh, why

am I telling (I, tell) you all this? You should see the film yourself.'

7229

Tip 26

Use the **simple present** (e. g. *he goes, I don't want*) for:
- summaries of stories, films and book reviews
- descriptions of characters in fictional texts
- comments on opinions/ideas
- your personal statement on your CV
- for talking about yourself and others; what you often do, what you like or don't like.

Use the **present progressive** (e. g. *he is going, I'm not going*) for actions and situations that are going on at the time. Remember, some verbs are not used in the progressive form: *believe, belong, know, like, need, own, seem.*

30 He didn't understand (Simple past or past progressive) ▶ GF (p. 155)

Complete with verbs in the simple past or past progressive.

Esra _wanted_ (want) to improve her English, so she _applied_ (apply) for a job as au pair in the USA.

She _didn't know_ (not know) much about her American host family,

but when she _arrived_ (arrive), all five members of her host family

were waiting (wait) to meet her. While Esra _was chatting_

(chat) to Mrs Jackson, Mr Jackson _picked_ (pick) up her large bag,

but Esra _said_ (say) loudly, 'Oh, no, Mr Jackson. You mustn't carry my bag.' So Mr Jackson

suddenly _put_ (put) the bag down again. Why _did Esra want_ (Esra, want) to carry the

heavy[3] bag herself? _Did she have_ (she, have) something important in her bag, or something that

might break? Mr Jackson _didn't say_ (not say) anything. When they _were walking_

(walk) out of the airport, Esra _thought_ (think), 'Why _did he put_ (he, put) my bag

down? Was it too heavy for him? What was the problem?' Do you know?

7230

Tip 27

Use the **simple past** (e. g. *went, didn't go*) for completed actions in the past, often with signal words - *yesterday, last year*, etc. Use it in stories or reports, or to talk about *when* something happened in the past. Make questions and negatives with **did**.

Use the **past progressive** (e. g. *was dancing, weren't eating*) for actions that were going on and not completed at a time in the past, for example, to describe a scene.

[1] drover [drəʊvə] *Viehhirte* [2] administrator [əd'mɪnɪstreɪtə] *Verwalter/in* [3] heavy ['hevɪ] *schwer*

31 Using different words (Synonyms)

a) Find and write pairs of words with similar meaning.

> afraid · allow · almost · awful · brilliant · close to · connect · dependable · discover · fantastic · find · impolite · latest · let · link · most modern · near · nearly · reliable · rescue · rude · sad · save · scared · strange · terrible · unhappy · unusual

afraid – scared, allow – let, almost – nearly, awful – terrible, brilliant – fantastic, close to – near,

connect – link, dependable – reliable, discover – find, impolite – rude, latest – most modern,

rescue – save, sad – unhappy, strange – unusual

b) Where can you use a synonym? Mark the word that you can replace. Then rewrite it.

1 Sylvie is training to be a bank clerk[1] in a bank near the town centre. ➔ *close to*

2 Her boss is very strict. He doesn't let his workers leave work early. ➔ *allow ... to leave ...*

3 Today Sylvie has almost finished her work. ➔ *nearly*

4 She is a good worker and very dependable. ➔ *reliable*

5 She would like to leave early, but she is afraid the boss will be angry. ➔ *scared*

6 The last time that someone wanted to leave early the boss was very impolite. ➔ *rude*

7 One day Sylvie found some documents – in the bin in her boss's office. ➔ *discovered*

7331

8 The next day, the boss asked Sylvie if she would like to leave early – how strange! ➔ *unusual*

32 Saying it differently (Changing sentence structure)

Use the word in brackets to express the meaning in a different way.

1 The phone rang while Mel was watching her favourite soap. (during)

   The phone rang during Mel's favourite soap.

2 It was her boyfriend. The last time she had seen him was three days ago. (for)

   She hadn't *seen him for three days.*

3 'Come to see the new film at the Majestic with me,' he said. (wanted)

   He *wanted her to come to see the new film at the Majestic with him.*

4 The cinema was full, but they were able to find some seats. (although)

   Although the cinema was full, they were able to find some seats.

5 The film wasn't as bad as the last one they had seen. (better)

   The film was better than the last one they had seen.

> **Tip 28**
>
> It is important to use your own words when you:
> • write a summary.
> • mediate what someone says.
> • answer questions about a text.
> • take notes from a written text.

[1] bank clerk [klɑːk] *Bankangestellte/r*

33 The flying doctors of Australia (RFDS) (Using linking words) ▸ WB (pp. 81–82)

Join two sentences with the linking word in brackets. Change the order of the sentences only where necessary.

Tip 29

Linking words are important in written English. They improve the style of your texts – and get you better marks in exams! Make sure that you use them whenever possible.

1 About 10% of Australians live far away from towns and cities. They can't get medical help easily. (so)

   About 10% of Australians live... cities, so they can't get medical help easily.

2 Before the RFDS started, many people died. Doctors could not reach them. (because)

   Before..., many people died because doctors could not reach them.

3 The Service is very well organized. It can reach people in over 80% of the country. (so)

   The Service is very well organized so it can reach people in over 80% of the country.

4 The RFDS has set up more than 20 bases[1] all over the country. Doctors can reach people quickly. (so that)

   The RFDS ... all over the country so that doctors can reach people quickly.

5 It is not easy to pass the tests and interviews. Lots of young people apply to the RFDS. (although)

   Although it is not easy to pass the tests and interviews, lots of young people apply to the RFDS.

6 The RFDS was started in about 1930. The RFDS is a 24-hour service. (which)

   The RFDS, which is a 24-hour service, was started in about 1930.

🖥 7433

34 Explaining words (Paraphrasing) ▸ WB (p. 79)

If you don't know the English word for what you want to say, you can paraphrase it. Paraphrasing is useful in mediation. You are talking to your English cousin about jobs and workplaces. Explain the following words in English. You can use these phrases:

- *It's someone/a person who... It's something that...*
- *It's something you use to... It's a place where...*
- *It's a (general word) that...*

I'd like to be a – erm, in German it's 'Regisseur'. *It's someone who knows a lot about film-making and directs films.*

1 Arbeitgeber/in: *It's a person who gives people jobs and pays them to work for the company.*

2 Bewerbungsschreiben: *It's a letter you send to a company when you want to get a job.*

3 Lebenslauf: *It's a paper you write yourself that tells people details about your education, work experience, etc.*

4 Führerschein: *It's something/the paper that shows that you can drive a car.*

🖥 7434

[1] base [beɪs] *Stützpunkt*

35 Making texts more interesting (Using adjectives)

a) *Choose three adjectives from the box that you could use in 1–4 below. Some adjectives fit into more than one list. Then add at least two more suitable adjectives to each list.*

boring · busy · clean · dangerous · exciting · healthy · interesting · noisy · polite · serious · quiet · reliable

1 a job: *boring, interesting, dangerous; difficult, useful*

2 a town/city: *busy, exciting, noisy; colourful, dangerous, old, modern*

3 the countryside[1]: *clean, quiet, healthy; beautiful, relaxing, calm, lonely*

4 a job candidate: *polite, serious, reliable; careful, nervous, interested*

b) *Write one or two sentences each about 1–4 in a). Use as many adjectives as you can from the lists.*

1 *I would like to have a job that's interesting and useful, not too difficult and not boring. I don't want a dangerous job.*

2 *Berlin is a busy, exciting city with lots of history. It is the mix of old and modern buildings that makes it so interesting. Like all cities it is busy and noisy in some parts.*

3 *We live in a town but my parents love the countryside, because it is quiet and relaxing. The air is clean and healthy too.*

4 *I hope I'll be a good job candidate one day. I'll try to be polite and serious at interviews. It's also important to be interested and not too nervous.*

36 She wanted to know ... (Indirect questions) ▶ GF (p. 170)

Jenny had an interview for a job as flight attendant[2]. She had some questions about the training course. What did she want to know? Report her questions.

Jenny asked/wanted to know ...

> **Tip 30**
> It is polite to use indirect questions in formal letters:
> *Could you please let me know whether/ when/where/who ...*
> Remember the backshift of tenses.

1 *how long the course was.*

2 *where the courses took place.*

3 *what the course hours were.*

4 *what she would learn on the course.*

5 *whether/if the instruction would be in English.*

6 *whether she would have to take any tests.*

7 *how many others would be on the course.*

7536

8 *whether she would get any money during training.*

1 *How long is the course?*
2 Where do the courses take place?
3 What are the course hours?
4 What will I learn on the course?
5 Will the instruction be in English?
6 Will I have to take any tests?
7 How many others will be on the course?
8 Will I get any money during training?

[1] countryside (*auf dem*) *Land*   [2] flight attendant ['flaɪt ə,tendənt] *Flugbegleiter/in*

Tip 31

Word order in English is different from German. It is always **Subject-Verb-Object**. Compare:
Since S. **left** *school* he has…
Seitdem S. die Schule **verließ**, *hat er…*

37 About Simon (Word order in subordinate clauses)

Write down the words of the subordinate clauses in the right order.

1 | Since | school | Simon | left |, he has been working as a trainee[1] in a local bank.

   <u>Since Simon left school,</u> he has been working…

2 Simon plays football for the local team, so | has to | he | regularly | twice a week | train |.

   … <u>he has to train regularly twice a week.</u>

3 If | well | he | works |, the manager lets him go home earlier.

   <u>If he works well</u>   , …

4 That's usually on the days when | has to | he | to | football training | go |.

   … <u>he has to go to football training.</u>

5 Sometimes the manager lets him leave early, | he | his work | hasn't finished | although |.

   … <u>although he hasn't finished his work.</u>

6 The manager lets him go early because | of the local team | he | too | is | a big supporter |.

   … <u>he is a big supporter of the local team too.</u>

Tip 32

Last but not least:
Always remember to read your texts carefully as soon as you finish them. Checking for mistakes is a very important part of any written task. Good luck!

38 A trip to New York (Correcting your text) ▸ WB (p. 82)

Correct Lina's e-mail to her online friend in Washington. Look for wrong words, wrong spelling (e.g. ~~planing~~) and grammar mistakes.

Hi Kelly!
Here we are in New York! It's so cool here. I really enjoyed ~~planing~~ our sightseeing tour ~~befor~~ we came and we've done ~~the most~~ of the things on my list. We've been in New York ~~since~~ two days. The ~~whether~~ was great yesterday, so we ~~have gone~~ up the Empire State Building. I ~~made~~ some pretty cool photos and I ~~heared many informations over~~ the details of the building. We all ~~have thought~~ that it was really ~~intresting~~. The ~~american peoples~~ are very friendly and ~~helpfull~~. They always ~~say~~ me what I want to know. New York isn't so far from Washington. Maybe I could ~~travell~~ down to Washington ~~with the~~ train to see you for a day or two. Would that be OK? ~~I'm calling~~ you this evening. ~~Than~~ you can tell me what you ~~mean~~. If I ~~would come~~ to visit you, I'm sure we ~~had~~ lots of fun! Lina

Correct

planning, before, most, for, weather, went, took, heard, a lot of information, about, thought,

interesting, American, people, helpful, tell, travel, by, I'll call, Then, think, came, would have

[1] trainee [treɪˈniː] *Auszubildende/r*

LISTENING SKILLS ▶ *p. 134*

SF REVISION   Listening

Vor dem Hören

– Frag dich, was du schon über das Thema weißt.
– Nutze Überschriften oder Bilder, um zu erahnen, was dich z.B. bei einer Geschichte erwarten könnte.
– Lies dir die Aufgaben auf deinem Aufgabenblatt genau durch und überlege, auf welche Informationen du dich konzentrieren musst.
– Bereite dich darauf vor, Notizen zu machen. Leg z.B. eine Tabelle oder Liste an.

Während des Hörens

Listening for gist:

Konzentriere dich beim ersten Hören auf allgemeine Informationen, z.B. die Personen (unterschiedliche Stimmen), das Thema, die Umgebung (Geräusche), die Atmosphäre (die Sprechweise der Leute).

Listening for detail:

– Mach dir noch einmal bewusst, worauf du genau achten willst (Hörauftrag), besonders bei Durchsagen (*announcements*), die du vielleicht nur einmal hören kannst.
– Gerate nicht in Panik, wenn du meinst, du hättest gerade etwas Wichtiges verpasst. Konzentriere dich auf die nächste wichtige Information.
– Lass dich nicht von anderen Einzelheiten oder Geräuschen ablenken.
– Mach nur kurze Notizen, z.B. Anfangsbuchstaben, Symbole oder Stichworte.
– Manche Signalwörter machen es dir leichter, den Hörtext zu verstehen.
  Aufzählung: **and**, **another**, **too**
  Gegensatz: **although**, **but**
  Grund, Folge: **because**, **so**, **so that**
  Vergleich: **larger/older/... than**, **as ... as**, **more**, **most**
  Reihenfolge: **before**, **after**, **then**, **next**, **later**, **when**, **at last**, **at the same time**

– Auch andere Details wie z.B. die Stimme, der Akzent oder der Tonfall des Sprechers oder der Sprecherin können dir helfen, Informationen über seine oder ihre Gefühle, Herkunft usw. zu bekommen.
– Unterteile Telefonnummern beim Aufschreiben: 0171 572 42 589.

Nach dem Hören

– Vervollständige deine Notizen sofort.
– Wenn du den Text ein zweites Mal hören kannst, konzentriere dich auf das, was du beim ersten Mal nicht genau verstanden hast.
– Schau dir noch einmal die Aufgabenstellung an. Sollst du die gehörten Informationen nutzen, um einen neuen Text zu schreiben? Dann achte auf die richtige Textform: Bericht, Beschreibung, ...

REVISION   Reading course – Zusammenfassung ▶ *pp. 136–137*

Working out the meaning of words

Das Nachschlagen unbekannter Wörter im Wörterbuch kostet Zeit und nimmt auf Dauer den Spaß am Lesen. Oft geht es auch ohne Wörterbuch:

1. Bilder und Zeichen erklären und ergänzen oft Dinge aus dem Text. Schau sie dir deshalb vor und nach dem Lesen genau an.
2. Manche Wörter erklären sich aus dem Textzusammenhang, z.B. *When we **reached** the station, Judy bought our tickets.*
3. Zu manchen englischen Wörtern fallen dir vielleicht deutsche, französische oder lateinische Wörter ein, die ähnlich geschrieben oder ausgesprochen werden, z.B. **excellent**, **millionaire**, **nation**, **reality**.
4. Es gibt neue Wörter, in denen du bekannte Teile entdeckst, z.B. **friendliness**, **helpless**, **understandable**, **gardener**, **tea bag**, **waiting room**.

Hmm, *ocean* sieht so aus wie „Ozean", oder?

Skimming and scanning

Beim **Skimming** überfliegst du einen Text schnell, um dir einen **Überblick** zu verschaffen.
Du willst dabei herausfinden, worum es in dem Text geht. Achte dabei auf

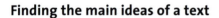

– die **Überschrift**,
– die **Zwischenüberschriften** und hervorgehobene Wörter oder Sätze,
– die **Bilder** und **Bildunterschriften**,
– den **ersten Satz** und den **letzten Satz** jedes Absatzes,
– **Grafiken**, **Statistiken** und die **Quelle** des Textes.

Beim **Scanning** suchst du nach **bestimmten Informationen**. Dazu suchst du den Text nach Schlüsselwörtern (*key words*) ab und liest nur dort genauer, wo du sie findest. Geh dabei so vor:

Schritt 1: Denk an die Schlüsselwörter und geh mit deinen Augen oder dem Finger schnell durch den Text, in breiten Schlingen wie bei einem „S" oder „Z" oder von oben nach unten wie bei einem „U". Die gesuchten Wörter werden dir sofort „ins Auge springen".

Schritt 2: Wenn das gesuchte Wort nicht im Text vorkommt, überlege dir andere, themenverwandte Wörter (z.B. lesson → school, subject) und suche nach diesen.

Finding the main ideas of a text

Zeitungsartikel, Berichte oder Kommentare verstehst du besser, wenn du ihre wesentlichen Aussagen erkennst und dir klar machst, wie sie zusammenhängen. Die wichtigsten Aussagen findest du so:

1. Jeder Text hat ein Thema mit mindestens einer Hauptaussage, z.B.: *Drinking soda is one of the worst things you can do to your health.* Diese Hauptaussage findest du oft im **ersten Absatz**.
2. Die Hauptaussage wird in der Regel durch weitere Aussagen bzw. Gedanken unterstützt, z.B.: *Experts agree that sugary soft drinks and fast food are the main reasons why so many American teenagers are fat.*
3. Diese weiteren Aussagen bzw. Gedanken werden oft durch Beispiele und Begründungen ergänzt, z.B.: *About 7% of the calories that they take in come from soft drinks alone.*

Careful reading

Schwierige Texte musst du besonders sorgfältig und konzentriert lesen, damit du alle darin enthaltenen Informationen und Gedanken verstehst.

1. Lies den Text genau. Welches sind seine wesentlichen Aussagen?
2. Manchmal musst du dir die Antwort auf eine Frage aus einzelnen Informationen erschließen, die du an verschiedenen Stellen im Text findest. Nimm zum Beispiel den Text auf S. 17 in deinem Schülerbuch: Warum ist in der Überschrift von einem „racist ideal" die Rede? Für die Antwort musst du mehrere Aussagen aus dem Text zusammentragen:

FACTS: • Zita Wallace and thousands of other mixed-race children with fair skin were taken from their Aboriginal families. • The government wanted them to forget their Aboriginal traditions and grow up like white children. • The children were hit if they spoke their own language. • They had to work all the time and didn't get any real education.

CONCLUSION: The government thought that Aboriginal culture had no value. The mixed-race children were forced to grow up among white people, but at the same time they were discriminated against.

Text types: fiction and non-fiction

Wenn du einen Text liest, ist es sinnvoll sich klar zu machen, ob er von einer vom Autor erdachten Welt handelt (*fictional text*, deutsch: Dichtung) oder sich mit der Wirklichkeit auseinandersetzt (*non-fictional text*, deutsch: Sachtext).

Fiktionale Texte sind z.B. Kurzgeschichten und Romane. Der Autor wählt Figuren (*characters*) aus und erzählt von ihren Gefühlen und Handlungen, von deren Motiven und Hintergründen. Die Handlungen finden in einem oder mehreren Handlungsrahmen statt, z.B. an einem Ort, zu einer bestimmten Zeit und unter bestimmten Umständen (*setting*). Die Ereignisse können aus verschiedenen Perspektiven erzählt werden (*point of view*). Oft verwendet der Autor für seine Geschichte eine anschauliche Sprache, z.B. ausschmückende Adjektive, Metaphern, Vergleiche, direkte Rede oder er lässt den Leser an den Gedanken seiner Figuren oder des Erzählers teilhaben.

Nicht-fiktionale Texte sind z.B. Berichte in Zeitungen, wissenschaftliche Artikel, Aufsätze oder Kommentare. Hier informiert der Autor über ein Thema der realen Welt oder nimmt Stellung dazu.

Es gibt auch Texte, die eine **Mischform** aus beiden Textarten sind.

MEDIATION SKILLS ▶ *p. 140*

SF REVISION Mediation

REVISION Wann muss ich zwischen zwei Sprachen vermitteln?

Manchmal musst du zwischen zwei Sprachen vermitteln. Das nennt man **mediation**.

1. Du gibst englische Informationen auf Deutsch weiter: Du fährst z.B. mit deiner Familie in die USA und deine Eltern oder Geschwister wollen wissen, was jemand in einem Café gesagt hat oder was an einer Informationstafel steht.

2. Du gibst deutsche Informationen auf Englisch weiter: Vielleicht ist bei dir zu Hause eine Austauschschülerin aus den USA oder Dänemark zu Gast, die kein Deutsch spricht und Hilfe braucht.

3. In schriftlichen Prüfungen musst du manchmal in einem englischen Text gezielt nach Informationen suchen und diese auf Deutsch wiedergeben. Oder du sollst Informationen aus einem deutschen Text auf Englisch wiedergeben.

Worauf muss ich bei *mediation* achten?

– Übersetze nicht alles wörtlich, sondern gib den Sinn wieder.
– Gib nur das Wesentliche weiter, lass Unwichtiges weg.
– Verwende kurze und einfache Sätze.
– Wenn du ein Wort nicht kennst, umschreibe es oder ersetze es durch ein anderes Wort.

You can go by train from Sydney to Perth. Trains go twice a week. The next train leaves Sydney on Saturday at 3 in the afternoon and arrives in Perth on Tuesday at 9 in the morning.

Was kann ich tun, wenn ich ein wichtiges Wort nicht kenne?

Vielleicht findest du es manchmal schwer, mündliche Aussagen oder schriftliche Textvorlagen in die andere Sprache zu übertragen, z.B. weil

– dein Wortschatz nicht ausreicht,
– dir bekannte Wörter „im Stress" nicht einfallen,
– spezielle Fachbegriffe auftauchen.

Manche Wörter kannst du umschreiben, z.B. mithilfe von Relativsätzen wie:

It's somebody/a person who ...
It's something that you use to ...
It's an animal that ...
It's a place that/where ...

Schau dir unten auch den Abschnitt zu Paraphrasing an.

Wir können mit dem Zug fahren, das dauert von Samstagnachmittag bis Dienstag früh.

SPEAKING AND WRITING SKILLS ▶ *p. 141*

SF REVISION Paraphrasing

Worum geht es beim Paraphrasing?

„Paraphrasing" bedeutet, etwas mit anderen Worten zu erklären. Das ist hilfreich, wenn dir ein bestimmtes Wort nicht einfällt oder wenn dein Gegenüber dich nicht verstanden hat. Paraphrasing ist auch besonders nützlich für **mediation** (▶ *Mediation, s.o.*).

Wie gehe ich beim Paraphrasing vor?

– Man kann mit einem Ausdruck umschreiben, der dieselbe Bedeutung hat: **'To wonder' is the same as 'to ask yourself'.**
Oder man sagt das Gegenteil: **'Alive' is the opposite of 'dead'.**
– Manchmal braucht man mehrere Wörter, z.B. wenn man etwas beschreibt oder erklären will, wie man etwas verwendet. Dabei verwendet man ein allgemeines Wort (**general word**) und nennt weitere Eigenschaften: **A skyscraper is a very tall building.**
– Oder du umschreibst das Wort mit **... is/are like ...** **A lodge is like a small house or cabin. You find it in the country.**
– Du kannst auch einen Relativsatz (**relative clause**) verwenden:
A ticket office is a shop where you can buy tickets for shows and concerts.

SF REVISION Brainstorming

Was ist Brainstorming und wofür ist es gut?

Bei vielen Aufgaben ist es nützlich, wenn du im ersten Schritt möglichst viele Ideen zum Thema sammelst. Beim Sammeln und beim Auswerten der Ideen helfen dir die folgenden Techniken.

Drei verschiedene Brainstorming-Techniken

Technik 1: Making a list

Schreib die Ideen so auf, wie sie dir einfallen, und zwar für jede Idee eine neue Zeile. Lies im zweiten Schritt alle deine Ideen durch. Überlege, welche Ideen davon für dein Thema sinnvoll sind und nummeriere sie nach Nützlichkeit.

Technik 2: Making a mind map

Leg eine Mindmap an. Überlege dafür, welche Oberbegriffe zu deinem Thema passen. Verwende unterschiedliche Farben für jeden Oberbegriff. Ergänze jede Idee, die zu einem Oberbegriff passt, auf einem Nebenast. Nimm dafür nur wichtige Schlüsselwörter. Du kannst statt Wörtern auch Symbole verwenden und Bilder ergänzen.

Technik 3: The 5 Ws

Schreib die Fragewörter Who? What? When? Where? Why? in eine Tabelle. Die Ideen, die dir zu der jeweiligen Frage kommen, werden darunter geschrieben.

Fantastic concert, isn't it?

SPEAKING COURSE – Zusammenfassung ▶ *pp. 142–143*

Having a conversation

Ein Gespräch beginnen

Ein Gespräch auf Englisch zu beginnen ist einfacher, als du vielleicht denkst. Es gibt immer mehrere Möglichkeiten:

– **Wenn du etwas erfragen willst** (z.B. den Weg oder die Uhrzeit) **oder um Hilfe bitten möchtest:** Excuse me, do you know … • Excuse me, can you tell me … • Excuse me, do you know where… • Could you help me, please?

– **Wenn du jemanden begrüßen möchtest oder kennen lernst:** Hi! • Hello! • Good morning. • (bei Erwachsenen) Good afternoon. Oft kann man das Gespräch dann mit einer allgemeinen Bemerkung weiterführen: Great day today! • Nice concert, isn't it? • … Oft hört man zur Begrüßung auch: How are you? oder How do you do? Das sind einfache Begrüßungsformeln, auf die keine Antwort erwartet wird. Am besten sagst du einfach: Fine, thanks. How about you?

– **Wenn du jemanden wiedertriffst:** Hi, …, how are things? • Hi, how is it going? • How are you? • Hi, good to see/meet you.

Ein Gespräch führen

Für den weiteren Verlauf des Gesprächs sind diese Wendungen nützlich:

– **Sich vorstellen:** By the way, my name's … • I'm …

– **Sich kennen lernen:** Have you … before? • Have you ever …? • What about you?

– **Sich bedanken/auf einen Dank reagieren:** Thanks! • Thanks for your help. • You're welcome.

– **Sich verabschieden:** See you tomorrow/next week. • Bye!

Und wenn du einmal etwas nicht verstanden hast, kannst du nachfragen:

Sorry, I didn't get that. • Sorry, can you say that again, please?

Asking for, confirming, giving information

Ein Gespräch ist mehr als nur der Austausch von Informationen; es kommt auch auf einen höflichen und angenehmen Ton an. Das gilt natürlich auch für Gespräche auf Englisch. Diese Wendungen können hilfreich sein:

– **Asking for information:** Oft beginnt man eine Anfrage oder Auskunft mit: Excuse me… • Excuse me, could you tell me, … • Would you mind telling me … • Sorry, I'd just like to know… • I'm not quite sure about … • Is it/Are they …? • Is it right that …? • Can I just ask … • Excuse me, I've just got a question … • Excuse me, do you think you could …?

– **Confirming information:** Wenn du nachfragen oder sichergehen möchtest, dass du etwas richtig verstanden hast, kannst du das z.B. so tun: Can I just confirm …? • Is it right that …? • Have I got that right …? • …, (is that) right? • Could you just say that again, please? Auch *question tags* drücken den Wunsch nach Bestätigung aus: This is the library, isn't it?

Denke auch daran, dich für die erhaltenen Informationen freundlich zu bedanken.

– **Giving information:** Auch wenn du selbst eine Auskunft erteilst, versuche freundlich und höflich zu sein, z.B. mit einer kurzen Einleitung: Sure. • Of course, no problem. • Well, just a second. • Give me a minute to think about it. Wenn du nicht weiter helfen kannst, drückst du dein Bedauern aus: Oh, I'm sorry, I don't know. • Sorry, I'm afraid I can't help you.

Giving an oral summary

Wenn du etwas, was du gehört, gesehen oder gelesen hast, für jemanden anderen zusammenfassen willst, tust du dies oft spontan. Du hast also nicht lange Zeit zum Überlegen und solltest auch nicht zu lange reden.

– Gib **nur das Wesentliche** des Inhalts wieder. Du brauchst dich nicht unbedingt an die chronologische Reihenfolge der Handlung zu halten: I watched that film … last night. • Yesterday I read that web article about … • I've recently come across that ad/article about … • I've just read that story about …

– Verwende das **Präsens** zum Nacherzählen: There's this kid … In this one scene he's running away from … then it starts raining … and he's trying … so she has to get out of the car …

– **Halte deine Meinung** zu dem betreffenden Film, Buch usw. **zurück**. Natürlich kannst du durch die Art und Weise, wie du erzählst, indirekt deinen Eindruck wiedergeben, z.B. durch den Ton deiner Stimme, deine Körpersprache und deine Wortwahl.

Having a discussion

Seine Meinung sagen und erklären

– **Expressing an opinion:** In einer Diskussion ist es gut, wenn du möglichst klar und deutlich sagst, was du zu einer bestimmten Frage denkst: I think … • I feel … • In my opinion …

– **Giving reasons and examples**: Es ist aber noch wichtiger, dass du Beispiele und Argumente nennst, die deine Meinung unterstützen – schließlich willst du deine Gesprächspartner ja überzeugen: because … • First … / Second … • For example … • Let me explain … • That's why …

Auf andere reagieren

– **Asking for clarification:** Manchmal ist es notwendig nachzuhaken: Could you say that again? • Sorry, but I don't understand what you mean.

– **Agreeing with someone:** Die Meinung eines anderen unterstützt du mit: I agree (with you/…). • That's a good point. • You're right.

– **Disagreeing with someone:** Oft widerspricht man nicht direkt, sondern leitet seine Reaktion z.B. mit Sorry, … ein. Zeig immer Respekt für die Meinung anderer: I don't think you can say … • I see what you mean but … • No, that's not right. • Sorry, I don't agree with you. • Yes, but …, • Well, I don't think you can say that … • Ah, come on, …

REVISION Writing course – Zusammenfassung ▶ *pp. 144–145*

> **The steps of writing**
>
> **1.** Brainstorming – Ideen sammeln und ordnen
> **2.** Schreiben. Dabei achte darauf,
> – deine Sätze zu verbinden und auszubauen (*Writing better sentences*),
> – deinen Text gut zu strukturieren (*Using paragraphs*),
> – bei einem Bericht die 5 Ws abzudecken (*Writing a report*),
> – bei einem Leserbrief an eine Zeitschrift eine höfliche Anrede und
>   Schlussformel zu verwenden (*Writing a letter to a magazine*).
> **3.** Deinen Text inhaltlich und sprachlich überprüfen (*Correcting your text*).

Writing better sentences

Linking words verbinden Sätze und machen sie interessanter. Verwende z.B.

– **Time phrases** wie at 7 o'clock, every morning, in the afternoon, a few minutes later, suddenly, then, next …,

– **Konjunktionen** wie although, and, because, but, so … that, that, when, while,

– **Relativpronomen** wie who, which und that.

Auch mit **Adjektiven** und **Adverbien** kannst du deine Sätze verbessern.

– **Adjektive** bestimmen Personen, Orte, Gegenstände oder Erlebnisse genauer und machen sie ebenfalls interessanter:
  The man looked into the room. → The young man looked into the empty room.

– Mit **Adverbien** kannst du beschreiben, wie jemand etwas macht: The young man looked nervously into the empty room.

Using paragraphs

Structuring a text

Einen Text versteht man viel besser, wenn er in Absätze gegliedert ist:

– eine Einleitung (**beginning**) – hier schreibst du, worum es geht,

– einen Hauptteil (**middle**) – hier schreibst du mehr über dein Thema,

– einen Schluss (**end**) – hier bringst du den Text zu einem interessanten Ende.

Am Anfang eines Absatzes sind kurze, einleitende Sätze (**topic sentences**) gut, die den Lesern sofort sagen, worum es geht, z. B.

– Orte: My trip to ... was fantastic. / ... is famous for ... / ... is a great place.

– Personen: ... is great/funny/interesting/clever/...

– Aktivitäten: ... is great fun. / Lots of people ... every day.

Wie kann ich meine Absätze interessant gestalten?

– Beginne mit einem interessanten Einstiegssatz: Guess what happened to me today! / Did I tell you that ...?

– Fang für jeden neuen Aspekt einen neuen Absatz an.

– Beende deinen Text mit einer Zusammenfassung oder etwas Persönlichem.

Linking ideas

Damit sich dein Text flüssig liest und beim Leser Interesse weckt, solltest du auf gute Übergange von einem Absatz zum nächsten achten. Die folgenden Formulierungen kannst du verwenden,

– um zu zeigen, wie dein Text aufgebaut ist: In the article, the writer describes how ... Firstly, he states that ... Secondly, ... Then he goes on to say that ... Another point he makes is that ... Finally, ...

– um etwas zu begründen: Because of / As a result of the growing population, ... ; ... had been in trouble with the police, so ...

– um zwei oder mehr Gedanken einander gegenüberzustellen: Although one could say that ..., I believe ... While most people would ..., the Prime Minister has said ... Serious scientists all say that ... However/But some politicians ...

– um Beispiele zu geben: This is true in a number of cases, for example / for instance / e.g. ...

– um Ergebnisse und Folgen zu erklären: As a consequence, / All in all, one can say that ... To sum up, I would like to say ...

Correcting your text

Lies jeden Text, den du geschrieben hast, mehrmals durch,

– um zu sehen, ob er vollständig und gut verständlich ist,

– um ihn auf Fehler zu überprüfen, z. B. **Rechtschreibfehler** *(spelling mistakes)* und **Grammatikfehler** *(grammar mistakes)*.

Spelling mistakes

Beachte folgende Regeln:

– Manche Wörter haben Buchstaben, die man nicht spricht, aber schreibt, z. B. talk, climb.

– Manchmal ändert sich die Schreibweise, wenn ein Wort eine Endung erhält, z. B. take → taking, terrible → terribly, lucky → luckily, try → tries (aber stay → stays), run → running, drop → dropped.

– Beim Plural tritt manchmal noch ein *-e* zum *-s*, z. B. church → churches.

Grammar mistakes

Diese Tipps helfen dir, typische Fehler zu vermeiden:

– Im **simple present** wird in der 3. Person Singular -s angehängt: she knows.

– **Unregelmäßige Verben**: Manche Verben bilden die Formen des *simple past* und des Partizip Perfekt *(past participle)* unregelmäßig. Die unregelmäßigen Formen musst du lernen, z. B. go – went – gone; buy – bought – bought. Die Liste steht im SB auf S. 256–257.

– **Verneinung**: Im *simple present* werden Vollverben mit don't/doesn't verneint, im *simple past* mit didn't.

– **Satzstellung**: Im Englischen gilt immer (auch im Nebensatz):

a) subject – verb – object (SVO): ... when I saw my brother.
                                    ... als ich meinen Bruder sah.

b) Orts- vor Zeitangabe: I bought a nice book in the city yesterday.

GF 4 REVISION Modals and their substitutes ▶ *pp. 164–165*

4.1 Modal auxiliaries

1 **Can** you **play** the piano?
2 – Yes, I **can**. / No, I **can't**.

3 Sue is good at drawing. <u>She</u> **should** study art.

4 **Could** you do the exercise? I **couldn't**.

5 **Can** we help you in the kitchen, Mum?
6 We **can** play tennis on Saturday if you like.

Modale Hilfsverben wie **can, may, must, should** drücken aus, was jemand tun **kann, darf, muss, soll** usw. Sie werden zusammen mit dem **Infinitiv eines Vollverbs** verwendet (1). Nur in Kurzantworten können sie allein stehen (2).
Weitere Merkmale modaler Hilfsverben:
– Sie haben nur <u>eine</u> Form, es gibt also keine Endungen auf *-s, -ing* oder *-ed* (3).
– Frage und Verneinung werden <u>ohne</u> *do/does/did* gebildet (4).
– Sie beziehen sich in der Regel auf die Gegenwart oder die Zukunft (5, 6).

4.2 Substitutes

1 I'd love to **be able to** speak Spanish.
2 **Being able to** speak Spanish must be great.
3 We **weren't allowed to** use a dictionary.

Modale Hilfsverben können **nicht alle Zeitformen** bilden. Daher gibt es zu bestimmten modalen Hilfsverben **Ersatzverben** mit ähnlicher Bedeutung, von denen man den Infinitiv (1), die *-ing*-Form (2) und alle Zeitformen (3, *simple past*) bilden kann.

„können": *can – (to) be able to*

My little brother **can/is able to** swim.
Tim **could/was able to** read when he was four.
I **could** smell fire, but I **couldn't** see any smoke.

Jacob **hasn't been able to** finish his essay.
I'm taking driving lessons, so next year I'**ll be able to** drive.

present:	*can* und *am/is/are able to*
past:	*could* und *was/were able to*
	could steht vor allem in verneinten Sätzen und Fragen sowie mit Verben der Wahrnehmung *(smell, see, hear, …)*.
present perfect:	*have/has been able to*
will-future:	*will/won't be able to*

„dürfen": *can, may – (to) be allowed to*

Can/May I have a sleepover on Friday, Mum?
We **aren't allowed to** stay up late in the week.
When I was a kid I **could/was allowed to** watch TV for an hour a day.
I'**ve** always **been allowed to** have pets.
Will you **be allowed to** go to the party on Friday?
Jeans **must not** be worn at this school.
At my school we'**re not allowed to** wear jeans.

present:	*can, may* und *am/is/are allowed to*
past:	*could* und *was/were allowed to*
present perfect:	*have/has been allowed to*
will-future:	*will/won't be allowed to*

! Für ausdrückliche **Verbote** wird *must not (mustn't)* oder *be not allowed to* verwendet.

„müssen": *must – (to) have to*

Teacher You **must** work harder, Noah.
His teacher says Noah **has to** work harder.
I **needn't** get up at 6 tomorrow. / I **don't have to** get up at 6 tomorrow.
I **had to** rewrite my essay.
We **didn't have to** wait long.
Lauren **has had to** go to the dentist's.
You **will have to** go to the dentist's too if you eat so many sweets.

present:	*must* und *have/has to* (*have/has to* ist häufiger als *must*)
	! **Verneinung:** *needn't* oder *don't/doesn't have to*
past:	*had to*
	! **Verneinung:** *didn't have to*
present perfect:	*have/has had to*
will-future:	*will/won't have to*

GF 8 The to-infinitive ▶ *pp. 172–173*

8.1 REVISION Verb + object + *to*-infinitive

Kim **helped** me to write my French essay.
Kim half mir, meinen französischen Aufsatz zu schreiben.

Sharon **asked** me not to use her photo.
Sharon bat mich, ihr Foto nicht zu verwenden.

Nach bestimmten Verben kann ein **Objekt + *to*-Infinitiv** stehen, z.B. ***ask/help/invite/teach sb. (not) to do sth.***

Nach den entsprechenden deutschen Verben steht meist ein Infinitiv mit „zu": ***jn. bitten/jm. helfen/…, etwas (nicht) zu tun.***

Grandma **expects** us to save our pocket money.
Oma erwartet, dass wir unser Taschengeld sparen.
Ed **would like** me to go to town with him.
Ed möchte, dass ich mit ihm in die Stadt fahre.
We **want** you to help us to clean up the beach.
Wir wollen, dass du uns hilfst, den Strand zu säubern

◄ Auch nach den Verben *cause, expect, tell, want, would like, would love* kann ein **Objekt + *to*-Infinitiv** stehen.
! Nach den entsprechenden deutschen Verben steht ein Nebensatz mit „dass". Auf die englischen Verben darf jedoch <u>kein</u> *that*-Satz folgen:
*Wir **wollen**, dass du uns hilfst. We **want** you to help us.*
Nicht: *We want ~~that you help~~ us.*

8.2 REVISION Question word + *to*-infinitive

We **don't know** what to do.
(… what we should/could do)
Wir wissen nicht, was wir tun sollen/könnten.
Let's **ask** someone how to get to the bus station.
…, wie wir zum Busbahnhof kommen (können).
Can you **tell** us which direction to take?
…, welche Richtung wir nehmen müssen?

Der *to*-Infinitiv steht oft nach einem **Fragewort** (*what, who, when, where, how* usw.) sowie nach *whether* („ob").
Er entspricht meist einem Nebensatz mit modalem Hilfsverb (*can, could, might, must, should*).
Die Kombination aus Fragewort und *to*-Infinitiv steht oft nach den Verben *ask, explain, find out, know, show, tell, wonder.*

8.3 The *to*-infinitive instead of a relative clause

1 I expect **the last (person)** to arrive will be Jo.
(… the last person who arrives …)
Tim was **the first (one)** to tell me the news.
(… the first one who told me …)
Sophie was **the only person/the only one** to say what she thought.
(… the only person/one who said …)
2 Who was **the youngest (girl or boy)** to take part in the competition?
(… the youngest girl or boy who took part …)

Der *to*-Infinitiv kann **anstelle eines Relativsatzes** stehen:
1 nach *the first, the last, the next, the only*

! Nach *the only* muss ein Nomen oder *one/ones* stehen.

2 nach einem Superlativ.

1 There are **clothes** to wash and **meals** to cook.
(… clothes that I/we must wash …)
James is **the person** to ask about computers.
(… the person who you should ask)
2 I'm looking for **someone** to share a flat with.
(… someone who I can share a flat with)
Lucy doesn't know **anybody** to play with.
(… anybody who she can/could play with)

Der *to*-Infinitiv kann **anstelle eines Relativsatzes <u>mit modalem Hilfsverb</u>** stehen:
1 nach einem **Nomen** (häufig nach *person, place, way*)

2 nach den Zusammensetzungen mit *some-, any-* und *no-* (*someone, something, somewhere, anything, nowhere* usw.).

GF 9 The gerund ▶ *pp. 174–175*

9.1 REVISION The gerund as subject and object

Subject	Object
Cycling is fun.	I love cycling.
Radfahren macht Spaß.	Ich liebe das Radfahren. / Ich fahre sehr gern Rad.

I like riding **motorbikes**.
Ich fahre gern Motorrad.
Cycling in the rain can be fun too.
Radfahren im Regen kann auch Spaß machen. /
Im Regen Rad zu fahren kann auch Spaß machen.
1 Nobody **enjoys** going to the dentist's.
Niemand geht gern zum Zahnarzt.
Imagine living in California!
Stell dir vor, in Kalifornien zu leben!
Tom **suggested** going for an ice cream.
Tom schlug vor, ein Eis essen zu gehen.

Wenn die *-ing*-Form eines Verbs die Funktion eines **Nomens** hat, wird sie **Gerundium** (*gerund*) genannt.
Das Gerundium kann **Subjekt** oder **Objekt** eines Satzes sein.

Wie ein Verb kann das Gerundium erweitert werden, z.B. durch ein Objekt (hier: *motorbikes*) oder eine Orts- oder Zeitangabe (hier: *in the rain*).

! Beachte:

◄ **1** Nach einigen Verben – z.B. *dislike, enjoy, finish, imagine, miss, practise, suggest* – muss ein weiteres Verb als Gerundium stehen:
*I **enjoy** going …; He **suggested** going …*
Anders als im Deutschen darf nach diesen Verben **kein Infinitiv** stehen!
Also nicht: *I ~~enjoy to go~~ …; He ~~suggested to go~~ …*

2 When it **started** raining / to rain we all went home.

Als es anfing zu regnen, gingen wir alle nach Haus.

Will **loves** doing / to do crazy things.

Will liebt es, verrückte Sachen zu machen.

◄ **2** Nach *begin/start, continue, hate, like, love, prefer* kann jedoch – <u>bei gleicher Bedeutung</u> – entweder ein Gerundium oder ein *to*-Infinitiv stehen.

3 I'll never **forget** talking to Robbie Williams.

Ich werde nie vergessen, wie ich mit Robbie Williams gesprochen habe.

I **forgot** to phone Grandpa. I'm sorry.

Ich habe vergessen, Opa anzurufen. Es tut mir leid.

◄ **3** Nach *forget, remember, stop, try* kann entweder ein Gerundium oder ein *to*-Infinitiv stehen, aber mit <u>unterschiedlicher Bedeutung</u>.

9.2 **REVISION The gerund after prepositions**

Boots are made for walking. So let's go!

... zum Wandern ...

In future, don't use my mobile without asking.

... ohne zu fragen

Nach einer Präposition *(by, for, of, without, ...)* muss ein Verb als Gerundium stehen.

GF 10 Participles ▶ *pp. 176–178*

10.1 **REVISION Participle forms**

Present participle (-*ing*):

| work | → | **working** | try | → | **trying** |
| dance | → | **dancing** | plan | → | **planning** |

Past participle, regular verbs (-*ed*):

| work | → | **worked** | try | → | **tried** |
| dance | → | **danced** | plan | → | **planned** |

Past participle, irregular verbs:

build	→	**built**	grow	→	**grown**
make	→	**made**	see	→	**seen**
teach	→	**taught**	write	→	**written**

◄ Das **Partizip Präsens** *(present participle)* bildet man durch Anhängen von **-*ing*** an den Infinitiv. Beachte die Besonderheiten bei der Schreibung.

◄ Das **Partizip Perfekt** *(past participle)* eines <u>regelmäßigen</u> Verbs wird durch Anhängen von **-*ed*** an den Infinitiv gebildet. Beachte auch hier die Besonderheiten bei der Schreibung.

<u>Unregelmäßige</u> Verben haben eigene *past participle*-Formen, die man einzeln lernen muss.

10.2 **REVISION Participle clauses instead of relative clauses**

The girl talking to Leo is my sister.

(The girl <u>who is talking</u> to Leo ...)

We often buy strawberries grown in California.

(... strawberries <u>which were grown</u> ...)

Partizipialsätze können Relativsätze verkürzen und werden daher oft anstelle von Relativsätzen verwendet.

◄ Das *present participle* entspricht einem Relativpronomen + Verb im **Aktiv**: *is talking*.

◄ Das *past participle* entspricht einem Relativpronomen + Verb im **Passiv**: *were grown*.

10.3 **The present participle after certain verbs**

Verb of perception + object + present participle			
	Verb	**Object**	**Present participle**
1 I	heard	people	shouting.
2 Rob	saw	two men	running out of the bank.
3 Sue	noticed	some men	getting into a blue car.
4 We	watched	the car	driving down the street.

1 Ich hörte Leute schreien.

2 Rob sah zwei Männer aus der Bank laufen.

3 Sue bemerkte, wie/dass einige Männer in ein blaues Auto stiegen.

4 Wir beobachteten, wie das Auto die Straße hinunterfuhr.

Mit einem **Verb der Wahrnehmung + Objekt + Partizip Präsens** sagt man, dass man etwas wahrnimmt, das gerade im Verlauf ist.

Verben der Wahrnehmung sind *feel, hear, listen to, notice, see, smell, watch.*

Im Deutschen verwendet man einen Infinitiv (1, 2) oder einen Nebensatz mit „wie" oder „dass" (3, 4).

10.4 Participle clauses instead of adverbial clauses

Time

Seeing Ellis Island for the first time, Ava was very excited.
(When Ava saw Ellis Island for the first time, …)
Als Ava zum ersten Mal Ellis Island sah, …
Arriving at the station, we went straight to the platform.
Als wir am Bahnhof ankamen, …
Asked to turn down his MP3 player, the boy started to shout
at the bus driver.   (When he was asked to turn down …)
Als er gebeten wurde, seinen MP3-Spieler leiser zu stellen, …

Partizipialsätze können **Nebensätze der Zeit**
oder **des Grundes** verkürzen.
Solche Partizipialsätze gehen oft dem Hauptsatz voran. Sie sind **typisch für das geschriebene Englisch**.
In gesprochenem Englisch werden meist
adverbiale Nebensätze bevorzugt.

Reason

Feeling tired, Emily took the bus home. (Because/Since she felt tired, …) Weil/Da sie sich müde fühlte, …
Warned by his wife, the man was able to escape.(Because he was warned by his wife, …)
Von seiner Frau gewarnt, … / Weil er … gewarnt wurde, …

Having + past participle

1 **Having passed** his exams, Mike applied for a job.
(After he had passed his exams, …)
Nachdem Mike seine Prüfungen bestanden hatte, …
2 **Having been** to Italy twice, we decided to go to Spain.
(Because/Since we had been to Italy twice, …)
Da wir schon zweimal in Italien gewesen waren, …
Not having seen the film, I bought the DVD.
(Because/Since I hadn't seen the film, …)
Da ich den Film nicht gesehen hatte, …

Partizipialsätze mit *having* + **Partizip Perfekt**
drücken immer **Vorzeitigkeit** aus.
Partizipialsätze mit *having* + **Partizip Perfekt**
entsprechen
1 einem adverbialen Nebensatz der **Zeit**,
meist mit *after* eingeleitet,
2 einem adverbialen Nebensatz des
Grundes.

Additional information

1a **Reading** a really boring book, I fell asleep.
Als/Weil ich ein wirklich langweiliges Buch las, …
1b **When/While reading** a really boring book,
I fell asleep. or I fell asleep **when/while
reading** a really boring book.
2a I saw a huge black dog **when/while walking**
down the street. (I was walking down the street)
Ich habe einen riesigen schwarzen Hund gesehen,
als/während ich die Straße hinunterging.
2b I saw a huge black dog **walking** down the street.
(= the dog was walking down the street)
Ich habe gesehen, wie ein riesiger schwarzer Hund
die Straße hinunterging.
3 **Although asked** to stop by the police, the
man drove on.

◄ Nicht immer ist eindeutig zu erkennen, ob ein Partizipialsatz
einem Nebensatz der Zeit oder einem Nebensatz des Grundes
entspricht (Satz **1a**).
Durch Voranstellen der **Konjunktion** *when* oder *while* macht
man deutlich, dass der Satz **zeitlich** zu verstehen ist (Satz **1b**).
◄ Wenn der Hauptsatz ein Objekt enthält (hier: *a huge black
dog*), gibt es oft große Bedeutungsunterschiede, je nachdem,
ob der Partizipialsatz mit Konjunktion (Satz **2a**) oder ohne
Konjunktion (Satz **2b**) verwendet wird.

◄ Partizipialsätze können auch durch andere Konjunktionen
eingeleitet werden, z.B. ***although, until, if, after, before***.

10.5 Participle clauses giving additional information

'I'll be back at 6,' he shouted, **banging** the door
behind him.
… rief er und knallte die Tür hinter sich zu.
Using a knife, he was able to open the door.
Indem er ein Messer benutzte, …
Lynn ran down the stairs, **losing** a shoe.
…, wobei sie einen Schuh verlor.

Partizipialsätze werden oft verwendet, um Zusatzinformationen zu geben oder die Begleitumstände
einer Handlung zu beschreiben. (Meist handelt es sich um
zeitgleich oder fast zeitgleich stattfindende Handlungen oder
Vorgänge.)
Im Deutschen steht meist ein Hauptsatz mit „und"
oder ein Nebensatz mit „indem" oder „wobei".

1 LISTENING Summer vacation

1 B; *2* B; *3* C; *4* C; *5* B; *6* B

2 LISTENING A day in the life of …

a) Why bushfires start

b) *1* F; *2* T; *3* F; *4* T; *5* F; *6* T; *7* T; *8* F; *9* T; *10* F; *11* F; *12* T

3 READING Sydney for everyone

a) Sydney's sights

b) Opening times, Sights information

c) *1* T; *2* F; *3* N; *4* T; *5* F; *6* N; *7* T; *8* F; *9* F; *10* N; *11* F; *12* T; *13* T; *14* N; *15* T

4a) WRITING A blog

Hi, friends!

Yesterday I arrived in this most fantastic city–Sydney! Today was our first day of sightseeing. It was pretty hot! First we went to see the famous Sydney Harbour Bridge. People were climbing it – but that's not for me! After that we went to The Rocks, that's an interesting part of town with fantastic old buildings. There are souvenir shops and cafés too. We went to the visitor centre and got some tourist brochures and maps.

My parents wanted to see the Opera House, so we went there next. You can take tours, but Dad said we didn't have enough time. In the afternoon we did a boat trip round the harbour and we sailed under the Bridge. That was better than climbing it!

Tomorrow will be a Bondi Beach day, so we'll have to 'slip, slop, slap'.

Log in again tomorrrow and hear all my news!

4b) WRITING A summary

The story is about Nina, her brother David and two friends who drive to Kakadu National Park to celebrate Nina's birthday. On the way they argue about the danger of saltwater crocodiles for tourists. David thinks they should be really careful because park rangers cannot give a guarantee for visitor safety, but Nina says David is too scared. That evening they celebrate at the campsite and next morning they leave for Jim Jim Falls. Nina and Mike want to go swimming there. When they are climbing over the rocks, David hurts his foot and can't continue. He is worried because they lose Nina and Mike. Cathy tries to comfort him. When the two come back, Nina is very quiet. At home she tells David about a huge saltie at the falls and how scared she was. She apologizes to David. She knows he was right and she was stupid. She asks him not to tell their parents.

5a) SPEAKING Travelling

1 Hi/Hello. What can you see on the Uluru tours, please?

2 What time does the tour start?

3 How long does the tour take?

4 Are the tourist guides Aborigines?

5 Do we get breakfast on the tour?

6 How much does the tour cost and what is included in the price?

7 I'd like to book the tour for tomorrow, for two adults and two teenagers, please.

5b) SPEAKING Travelling

Picture A shows a scene in the outback with two people, a white camping bus on the right and a small white tent in the foreground on the left. The man is sitting on the front of the bus looking at the sky, and the woman is sitting on the camping chair. The sky is bright red, so maybe the sun is going down. There's nothing in the background, only red earth for miles. There's nothing green, no plants or bushes. The people look very relaxed. Maybe they're tired after a hot day of driving. It seems to be very lonely and quiet, maybe even boring. They're both wearing shorts, so it is probably still hot. They've put up the tent before it gets dark.

5c) SPEAKING Travelling

I think I would prefer a beach holiday in Australia because the outback is maybe good for people who love adventure but not for people who want to have fun on holiday. Maybe the beaches are crowded, but I love swimming and playing ball games on the beach. I would like to learn to surf too. I like going to discos and I would love the evening beach parties. I like sightseeing, museums, theme parks and shopping. I could do all those things on a beach holiday. I could also practise my English and make new friends.

I would like to make a short trip to the outback, maybe just for two or three days. In the outback the scenery is unique, but maybe it gets boring when you see it all day. I would like to meet some Aborigines and talk to them about their culture and their art.

I'm also interested in the animals in the outback. Maybe I could see a dangerous snake or other animals that live there.

6 MEDIATION Berlin tours

Alpha tours – Berlin: tours by bus, bike or on foot, every day; groups – all sizes; modern buses and new bikes; highlights – Brandenburg Gate, Checkpoint Charlie, small part of the Berlin Wall, TV tower, Berlin Cathedral, Charlottenburg Palace and more; tours morning, afternoon and evening, stops and meal included on day tours, guides speak foreign languages, see website for details

Skills Check 2 Lösungen/Musterlösungen

1 LISTENING First day at work
1 B; *2* A; *3* B; *4* A; *5* B; *6* B; *7* C; *8* A

2 READING Jobs
a) Young people describing jobs that they do
b) *1* D; *2* A; *3* B; *4* F; *5* E
c) *1* Nick *2* Sam *3* Lauren *4* Lucy *5* Nick *6* Adam
   7 Sam *8* Sam

3 WRITING A formal letter
...

Dear Mr Sutton
I read your advertisement in the Cornish Daily Post of ...
about job vacancies for German-speaking students in
Cornish hotels this summer. I would like to apply, but I
have a few questions first:
What kind of work would I have to do? In which towns
are your hotels? How many hours do students work each
day/week? How much is the pay? How much free time
would I have and when? Would accommodation and
meals be free?
I already have some work experience in a German hotel
kitchen. I am a friendly, reliable person and a good team
worker. I would like to work some time abroad and
improve my English.
I look forward to hearing from you.
Yours sincerely...

4 WRITING Your CV
Individual answer: please check your answer with the
CV and CV tips in your student's book on pp. 38–39.

5 WRITING An informal letter
Hi ...!
It was good to hear from you! Thanks for sending the ad
about hotel jobs. Yes, I'm very interested! Let me tell you
about it.
Well, my parents think that working away from home
would be good for me – and for my English – but they
want to know more about the jobs. So I've written to the
manager. I asked about the kind of work, pay, free time,
accommodation, etc. If it sounds OK, I'll apply.
I'd really like to have some work experience in the UK. It
would look good on my CV. I might make some new
friends and maybe I could visit you in my free time.
But it may not be very exciting. I expect the work will be
quite hard, the pay will be terrible and there won't be
much free time ...
I'll write again soon and let you know.
Love ...

6a) SPEAKING Jobs and work experience
Picture 1 shows a tourist guide on a London sightseeing
bus, telling tourists about the history of the city and its
buildings. Maybe the tourists aren't listening to
everything he says. I think it's quite a good job because
you are mostly outside and you meet a lot of people. But
it's the same routine every day, like most jobs. The guide
probably says exactly the same things to all his tourist
groups, and he does the same tour at the same time
every day. He probably feels bored, but he always has to
be friendly.

Picture 2 shows office staff working at their computers
in a large, open-plan office. They are probably not very
happy that they have to share such a large office. It think
it's hard to work there when there are so many people in
one room. There's always something happening and
there's always some background noise, people
telephoning, chatting, walking past you, telephones
ringing, etc. The workers are never private. Everybody
sees and hears what they do – the boss too.
I would prefer the job of the tourist guide because I
think it's more relaxing riding around London in a bus
than looking at a computer screen all day.

6b) SPEAKING Jobs and work experience
I think work experience is very important. You have to be
punctual, reliable, confident and hard-working. You
learn skills that are important for the world of work like
organisation, telephone skills, team work, maybe new
computer skills.
Last year I worked at a petrol station at the weekends. I
had to work in the shop too. I liked chatting to the people
there, but it was really boring most of the time. I like to
be with people.
I haven't got a job at the moment because I have to work
hard for school now.
My favourite school subjects are Maths and Physics.
They are both subjects that really interest me, and my
grades are good.
When I leave school I'd like to travel abroad and see how
other people live. I'd like to go to South America, and
some countries in Asia. After that I think I'd like to get a
place at university and maybe study Physics. It would be
good to go to the UK or the US for a work placement.
Then I could really improve my English.

7 MEDIATION Small ads
1 Job in a café: can work three hours morning or
   afternoon, have to work in kitchen and café preparing
   vegetables, doing tables, serving ice cream and cakes
   in garden, good pay
2 Job in hotel (near cathedral): can work part-time or
   hourly, have to answer phone calls in English and look
   after English-speaking guests, needn't have
   experience of hotel work, above average pay
3 Job with American family: have to look after young
   children, afternoons, don't have to do housework,
   needn't have a driving licence
4 Job giving English conversation classes to small
   groups: two hours twice a week mornings, don't have
   to speak German